I0041162

the global **leadership** lookout

CCBS Press

Cross Cultural Business Skills Minor

the Global Leadership Lookout

Comparative studies on leadership practices in eighteen nations

Amsterdam University
of Applied Sciences

ISBN: 978-90-79646-40-1
NUR: 812

CCBS-Press
First edition 2018
Editorial manager: Aynur Doğan
Series editor: Sander Schroevers
Assistant lecturers: Kalin Tsanov, Natalia Kempny, Susanne Koelman, Angeline van Wijk
Academic English and citations editor: Isabella Venter, University of Pretoria, South Africa
CCBS is an elective course at the Amsterdam University of Applied Sciences (HvA)
Inner and cover design: Sander Schroevers, Jaguar Print
Logo design: Erica Frank, Designer Gráfico, Vitória, Espirito Santo, Brazil
Cover graphic: Evgeniy Bulatnikov, Ukraine

Text copyright: Alexander Dewell, Andrej Karamešić, Anke ten Barge, Anouk Duurland, Anouk Verburg, Arjan Möller, Bart de Mooij, Benjamin Balindong, Bob Driessen, Bob Kleingeld, Cees Spooren, Charlotte Le Meur, Charlotte ten Berge, Danique Happel, 王丹妮 (wáng dān nī), Dominique Gunnink, Efecan Uygur, Elisia Piperni, Elize Wester, Elske Wismeier, Eve Lochhead, Farrez Hussainali, Feyaaz Hussainali, Fikri El Aarkoubi, Floris Valk, Frank Eriks, Frederike van den Brande, Geraldine van Dillewijn, Giles Agbenyoh, Huib de Jong, Ilias Fatah, Jenny Vuong, Jens Smit, Jeroen Dekker, Jesse Gerritsen, Jill Hoost, Joost van Vliet, Juno Beckers, Kalok Man, Kilian Schrijvers, Laila Notkamp, Lars Smithuis , Любомир Томов (Lubomir Tomov), Mahesh Vasnani, Maika van der Hulst, Marelle Schimmel, Marjolein Hessels, Marta Diaz Ximenez, Max Veltman, नायला सिद्दीकी (Nayaelah Siddiqui), Niek Jacobsen, Noa Schuitemaker, Patrick Dell, Полина Бурмистрова (Polina Burmistrova), Raymon Foget, Robbert Pieete, Robert Mićić, Robin Bol, Salman Hassan, رزقي سمير (Samir Rezgui), Samuël Boerhoop, Sebas Mak, Sue-hayne Jamanika, Thomas van Cappellen, Tirsa Haaswijk, Vincent Rosing, Wakas Khawaja and Wiebe de Boer.

Copyright © CCBS-Press and the Hogeschool van Amsterdam, 2018
All rights reserved. No part of this book may be reproduced, stored in a database or retrieval system, or published in any form or in any way, electronically, mechanically, by print, photo copy, scan or any other means without prior written permission from the editor: s.schroevers@hva.nl In so far as the making of copies from this edition is allowed on the basis of Article 16h-16m of the Auteurswet 1912 jo., the Decree of the 27th of November 2002, Bulletin of Acts and Decrees 575, the legally due compensation should be paid to Stichting Reprorecht (P.O. Box 3060, 2130 KB Hoofddorp, The Netherlands). For the inclusion of excerpts from this edition in a collection, reader and other collections of works (Art. 16 of the Copyright Act 1912) please refer to the editor. The greatest care has been taken in compiling this book. However, no responsibility can be accepted by the respective authors, the editorial board or the Hogeschool van Amsterdam for the accuracy of the information presented. All material has been scanned on plagiarism on Ephorus beforehand, any inadvertent omissions can be rectified in future editions. In the preparation of this book every effort was made to avoid the use of actual company names or trade names. If any has been used inadvertently, the editor will change it in any future reprint if they are notified. Where opinion is expressed, it is that of individual authors and does not necessarily coincide with the views of the Hogeschool van Amsterdam.

A CIP catalogue record for this book is available from the British Library, the Library of Congress, and the Netherlands Deposit Collection of the royal library in The Hague. Books from this series can be ordered via **GooglePlay** as an e-book, or as a free pdf download through the website: www.minorccbs.com.

Table of Contents

About CCBS

Since 2010, Cross Cultural Business Skills (CCBS) aims to educate bachelor students in the fundamentals of cross-cultural business skills and selected methodologies. CCBS is an elective course ('minor') initiated by prof. Sander Schroevers, and taught together with Aynur Doğan [MA], at the Amsterdam University of Applied Sciences (Netherlands).

Educational approach
At CCBS we believe that effective learning takes place through engaging in first-hand experiences. We challenge our students to produce new knowledge from a localised perspective. They often research in an unknown language, alphabet or cultural legacy which facilitates our students in developing meaningful skills for today's interconnected world. Our main objective is to co-create country-specific bodies of knowledge. We do so through expert-interviews (video and audio) with natives, and through in-depth analyses of local academic and trade literature.
In order to create a truly international classroom experience, we try to host students from across the globe. We attempt to connect our students with representatives of the business, media and diplomatic communities, during home-staged professional symposia. All CCBS-learning materials (print, digital and video) are 100% custom-tailored. We care about having the university's highest evaluation scores and have done so for many semesters now.
We therefore try to frame our lessons to be 'eye-popping', our work-shops to be clarifying and hands-on, and our social events to be warm and inclusive.
In short, let's do everything possible to make school cool!

About CCBS global-fact-tank
CCBS global fact tank is an ongoing academic research project from the Amsterdam University of Applied Sciences that informs on cross-cultural business topics. Every six months, CCBS researchers survey C-level executives around the world. Our key focuses cover the following five areas of activity: management, meetings, leadership, recruitment and business presentations. Since its first international poll in 2012, the CCBS global-fact-tank has conducted interviews in 74 trade nations, with thousands of professionals.

Preface

Welcome to an intercultural benchmark on local leadership practices in no less than eighteen countries. Our world is internationalising at a fast pace, and more and more of us choose to find work elsewhere. As a result, we find ourselves confronted with culturally diverse management expectations. After working on this series, we now understand how knowledge of such local leadership conventions, can represent an important competitive advantage. This book is the result of the collaborative research of seventy-six participants to the 'Cross-Cultural Business Skills' elective (minor) course. They have explored what leadership entails by doing a one semester - desk and field research. Together they have asked thousands of business professionals in selected countries on their preferred managing practices. The result of their efforts constitutes a relevant reference. We are grateful that this wonderful group can now share their gathered knowledge with interested people from around our world.

We first and foremost would like to thank all individual co-authors for their thoughtful research and constructive writing for this very first edition of 'the Global Leadership Lookout'. Additionally, we would like to express our deep appreciation to all survey correspondents and interviewees who helped, despite their busy schedules, to make this innovative and applied way of education possible. We also gratefully acknowledge that this book would not have been here, without the engagement of Part-time Academy Director Hans Seubring-Vierveyzer. Then we owe a debt of gratitude to Isabella Venter for her hard work in authenticating all our academic sources. Furthermore we would like to thank Kalin Tsanov, Natalia Kempny, Susanne Koelman and Angeline van Wijk for their much-appreciated assistance. Lastly, we take responsibility for any errors that may have inadvertently found their way into this book. May we close here, by wishing you all a remarkable read?

Sander Schroevers & Aynur Doğan

Consultation methodology

For the information in this book, results from three main data collection methods were applied. Firstly, insights around cultural aspects of leadership were gathered by conducting country-specific literature research, in both scholarly articles in journals, and preferably in-country books, and thus creating an extensive foundation for the validity of this book and its contents. Secondly, this quantitative research was strengthened by a global online survey about leadership (CCBS Survey, 2018). To select qualified respondents for the survey, expert sampling was used. Furthermore, snowballing techniques were used because the target population is difficult to get in touch with. In total over 2,200 respondents participated after visiting our survey link, but more than half were not used because of stopping the survey too early, or their background or IP-address did not match our target group.

The survey was created in English and translated by competent bilinguals who were either research collaborators or were supervised by them. The present study made use of translations into Arabic, French, German, Italian, Korean, Portuguese, Russian, Slovenian and Spanish. Checks on translation accuracy were completed by back-translation or parallel translations, where possible. The English version was used in eight countries. The questionnaire comprised of 27 items, with multiple-choice and open questions, providing descriptive information on the national views on leadership). The multiple-choice responses were made on five-point Likert scales, anchored by terms ranging from 'not at all' to 'a lot'.

All qualitative data provided comprehensive knowledge on the subject of local leadership cultures. The current multinational survey and interviewing was conducted between 13 February and 11 May 2018. Results using the outcome have not been reported prior to the present study.

Thirdly, in addition to the survey respondents, a selection of 47 leadership experts has been interviewed. These interviews lasted 20-40 minutes on average and were video and audio recorded and transcribed (a selection of these will be published on the YouTube and SoundCloud channels of CCBS minor).

Baas

Генеральный Директор

Geschäftsführerin

Bölüm Başkanı

Executive Vice President

Patrão

Økonomidirektør

Direttore Generale

CEO

회장님

Dyrektor

Président Directeur Géneral

Consejero Delegado

Τομεαρχης

MAIN DUDE

Country profiles

Sander Schroevers

I just checked on Amazon.com for the number of books using the word 'leader' in their titles and saw an astounding 60,000 results. A quick search on ProQuest (a database we recommend for scholarly journals), resulted in almost a million hits on the subject of 'leadership'. But as the Global Leadership and Organizational Behavior Effectiveness (GLOBE) Research Program noted, "that to date 90% of leadership literature reflects US based research and theory". Estimates like this keep us in the dark how effective all this leadership knowledge is across national frontiers. Seeing that the number of countries expands, so do the differences... I have always liked that Peter Drucker quote: "Management is doing things right; leadership is doing the right things.". The point being that leadership partly focuses on the people-side of business, while management is often about systems and processes. Research has proven to us that leaders' communication styles are influenced by the geographical region in which they operate. Regrettably, some business leaders overlook local managerial and cultural practices, acquiescing in management-styles that have been grounded in Western concepts, that may undermine performance of an organisation.

And as ineffective managers risk organisations costing large sums of direct and indirect costs, we nowadays see human resource professionals as well as senior executives pursuing more localised leadership strategies.

Chapter makeup

This book consists of 18 country chapters, each describing the local leadership perspective. All country profiles have been written in a standard format as to create a clear overview of the cultural features, while painting a contrast when comparing these leadership profiles to each other. Most of the eighteen country profiles in this book contain the following sections:

- *Country introduction,*
- *How the indigene characterise leaders,*
- *Survey results and what local respondents say,*

- *An in-country literature review,*
- *A transcribed telephone interview with a local leadership scholar,*
- *A summarised video interview with a local cross-cultural trainer,*
- *A description of an in-country best-selling book on leadership,*
- *Understanding hierarchy in that country,*
- *How to achieve leadership empathy in that particular culture.*

Allow me to shortly introduce some of the sections to you here;

Local leadership analysis

The more I work abroad, the more I realise that it takes something else than just a survey to categorise national cultures by. There seem to be so many local variations and nuances, that simply do not fit into such constructs. But these nevertheless may have a substantial influence on how effective one can operate in a particular country. There are a great many books that have western authors explaining countries, but the local perspective often seems missing. This localised focus became pivotal to our approach of investigating country-specific leadership characteristics. Which we try to accomplish by introducing such sections as: (i) survey-results and what local respondents say, (ii) an in-country literature review, (iii) a local leadership scholar, (iv) a local cross-cultural trainer, (v) an in-country best-selling book on leadership, that all specifically draw on indigenous leadership research. For some teams researching in other languages or even scripts, has been challenging but allowed for rich ethnographic descriptions with the aim of discovering how leadership is enacted in eighteen selected markets.

Understanding hierarchy in a country

Many of the western leadership trends in the twentieth century have been about abandoning hierarchical command-and-control processes. Management literature and business school education started introducing a more egalitarian and facilitative style of leadership. We started to see open-plan office architecture, and 360-degree feedback. There is a striking disconnect between cultures on attitude toward authority. In India the teaching staff is addressed with Madam or Sir, and I occasionally saw students stand up when their 'senior-lecturer' entered the classroom. In my own Dutch course (CCBS - authoring this book) local students address me by my first name, and at times feel free to contradict me in front of the class. Perhaps inspired by this, we asked about a thousand qualified respondents in our global survey if they expected to be addressed by first name rather than by title. For the selected eighteen national cultures, the following average scores were obtained;

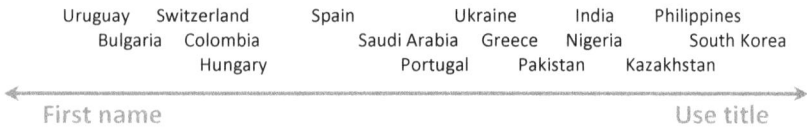

Uruguay	Switzerland		Spain		Ukraine	India	Philippines
	Bulgaria	Colombia		Saudi Arabia	Greece	Nigeria	South Korea
		Hungary			Portugal	Pakistan	Kazakhstan

First name ← → Use title

Figure: Employees can address their leader in this country by the first name.

Relational hierarchy

Eight out of ten Swiss survey participants admit that employees greet their leaders by the first name (CCBS Survey, 2017). This low level of hierarchy results in equal harmonious relationships between superior and employee, based on trust. Having a clear notion of someone's relative level of authority is of critical importance in, for instance, a country like Korea. It determines how colleagues interact with each other, including choosing amongst the many different linguistic levels of politeness. Organisations tend to have a great many more levels of management, and corresponding forms of address. The informal way of doing business in for instance Australia might confuse the average Korean. Especially those who have risen to high positions in their organisations, who often are accustomed to a V.I.P. treatment.

Power Distance

The words *Hierarchy* and *Power Distance* are often used as equivalent expressions. The latter being defined as "the degree to which members of an organization or society expect and agree that power should be stratified and concentrated at higher levels of an organization or government" (House & Javidan, 2004, p. 12). Countries that have scored high Power Distance values in, for instance, the Hofstede or Trompenaars research, believe that power dispenses agreement, social order, and role stability, and therefore power should be concentrated at higher levels. In high power-distance cultures, paternalism characterizes leader-subordinate relationships, where a leader will assume the role of a parent and feel obligated to provide support and protection to subordinates under his or her care (Yan & Hunt, 2005).

Many of the eighteen country profiles in this book make mention of a country's Power Distance Index score (PDI) by Dutch cultural scientist Geert Hofstede. However, just a value score number will not yet explain how hierarchy is understood in a particular culture. For example, even though Greece and South Korea both have equally high PDI values (of 60), leadership is enacted in a fundamentally different way in both countries. In this book we therefore try to remedy such cultural contingencies through culture-specific qualitative research, like interviewing local cultural intelligence experts.

How to achieve leadership empathy

Under this header each country profile will focus on a people-oriented leadership requirement: empathy. We here define empathy as a leader's capacity to relate to the feelings and experiences of others. Empathy as such, is broader than sympathy, and several researchers believe empathy to be a key part of emotional intelligence, and a critical element to being an effective leader (Bar-On & Parker, 2000). The successfully building and maintaining relationships, is a fundamental managerial skill. The point however is that according to the Center for Creative Leadership in some cultures empathy is more important to job performance than others (Gentry, Weber, & Sadri, 2016). Additionally, the way empathic emotion is expressed is subject to considerable local variations and nuances from country to country. It touches upon a leader's understanding of *role requirement*. Several questions of our online survey (CCBS Survey, 2018) refer to what particular expectations respondents have on this matter. Furthermore, each country team has tried to interview local experts, scholars and cross-cultural trainers on country-specific ways of demonstrating empathy in order to be effective. To give an example: in Nordic countries empathy is partly established by a low-key and modest behaviour, where for instance Latin countries much prefer a warm, personal and 'simpatico' approach. Koreans on the other hand value a courteous leader that protects face. How to connect with people seems to depend on cultural background, and an ability to be empathetic is especially important for leaders working across cultural boundaries (Alon & Higgins, 2005). The results of our CCBS Survey (2018) reflect this finding, as for all eighteen cultures discussed in this book, a large majority agreed to the statement that a manager should actively spend time on the personal well-being of team members. When comparing the actual country scores (Dell, Eriks, 2018), South Korea and Bulgaria realise significantly lower on empathy compared to countries like for instance Uruguay, Spain and Portugal. As generally Bulgarian and South Korean leaders prefer to keep more personal distance from their employees. But note that having empathy, is not the same as demonstrating empathy; as staff expectations may vary considerably per national culture in areas like: (i) the amount of verbal attention employees require, (ii) the expected praise and encouragement by staff, or for instance (iii) the daily routine of managers. When managers increase their awareness of this empathic cultural context, it often has a direct impact on performance, the organisational climate and more productive working relations between leaders and employees.

Concluding
It was Darwin who has shown us the supreme value of diversity. The growing cultural diversity of today's workforce, and the global locations of organisations, transforms the way we lead teams. This calls for leaders with an ability to decode cultural differences and to adjust their leadership-style to fit the relevant context. In sum, I hope that our findings may lead to a richer leadership literature and allow professional leaders to recalibrate their skills and mindsets and use them as an advantage.

Bulgaria

Lubomir Tomov (Любомир Томов), Noa Schuitemaker & Robert Mičić

Bulgaria (България) is located in south-eastern Europe and shares its national borders with Greece, the Republic of Macedonia, Romania, Serbia and Turkey. Bulgaria joined the EU over a decade ago, after being a socialist country until 1989. The currency used is the Bulgarian Lev (Лев), with 1 Lev (лв) being the equivalent of approximately 0.63 US Dollars. The country covers a surface area of just over a hundred thousand square kilometres, with a population of over 7 million citizens (OWNO, 2015; The World Bank Group, 2018). Around two-thirds of the population lives in urban areas, with over a million citizens living in the capital city, Sofia. The official language of the country is Bulgarian, which is spoken by just over two-thirds of the population, and the alphabet used is Cyrillic. The most widely spread religion in Bulgaria is Eastern Orthodox Christianity, with over half of the population practising it (Bulgarian Presidency of the Council of the European Union, n.d.).

Bulgaria has an open market economy, which has shown considerable growth for the country in the past (The World Bank Group, 2018). However, the per-capita income is still among the lowest in the EU (Eurostat, 2017). The economic growth is very sensitive to changes in external market conditions, due to the reliance on energy imports from Russia and foreign demand in Bulgarian export (Abbasova, 2017; Novinite JSC., 2016; Shiryaevskaya, 2016).

How the Bulgarians characterise leaders

In Bulgaria, the typical leader tends to be more authoritarian or autocratic, because of the high power-distance of the Bulgarian culture (Minkov, 2010). For this reason, it is expected of leaders to make firm company decisions and give clear orders. Employees have to respect their authority and follow orders accordingly (CCBS Survey, 2018). A successful leader, in the eyes of the Bulgarians, is one who displays strong and masculine personality traits (Ignatov, 2 April 2018). Therefore, the typical leader is expected to exude confidence, which remains unfazed during times of difficulties. Furthermore, it is customary for Bulgarian leaders to be dismissive when given feedback, showing a certain level of arrogance (Ignatov, 2 April 2018). Although rank and hierarchy are of great importance in the Bulgarian management culture, individual rights are just as significant (Bobina, Sabotinova & Grachev, 2017). More modern entrepreneurial companies take employee initiatives into consideration when deciding the best course of action (AUBG, 2014). Furthermore, Bulgaria is highly risk-aversive, which entails a need for strict rules, a rigid code of belief and an intolerance of unorthodox behaviours and ideas (Minkov, 2010). Normally, this would also mean that punctuality is very important to Bulgarian leaders. However, professionals have a more flexible approach to prioritising and time-management. With industry sectors becoming more and more international, they still tend to adhere to a strict schedule (CCBS Survey, 2018).

Finally, it is extremely important for leaders to form close, personal relations with their business partners and immediate followers (Ignatov, 2 April 2018). Deciding on a deal or contract could take a long time in Bulgaria as leaders are often seen as tough negotiators (Kicheva, 2017). For this reason, initial meetings may only entail getting to know business partners on a personal level. Engaging in non-formal, social interactions when doing business is quite common.

Survey results and what local respondents say

Bulgarians see tremendous value in managerial decisions and show respect for authority. Over 60% of the CCBS Survey (2018) respondents agree with the statement: "Management decisions are not easy to be changed after it has already been made." The same group also indicates that missing a deadline is seen as a failure. The majority of respondents support the idea of confronting team members during staff meetings in order to encourage them to obtain the wanted results (CCBS Survey, 2018). Joro Ignatov shares that: *"Leadership in Bulgaria is very task-oriented"* (2 April 2018). Fifty percent of respondents consider the personal distance from top management as important, as to maintain a good level of respect. Moreover, leaders prefer to hear criticism in an indirect manner. Dimitur Betchev, an export professional, states that: *"...people do not evaluate positively critics [sic]"* (CCBS Survey, 2018). Additionally, organisations may provide leaders with respectable office spaces and transportation in accordance with their position (CCBS Survey, 2018). According to Kicheva (2017), most leadership styles reflect the influence of socialism, which managers from older generations have incorporated over the years (Mayhew, 2011). Georgi Pavlov, a Bulgarian HR specialist, supports this argument by saying: *"Leadership in Bulgaria is still influenced by the socialism [sic]"* (CCBS Survey, 2018). When asked if employees may bend the rules in order to improve their performance, over sixty percent of respondents answer affirmatively. The CCBS Survey (2018) indicates that high value is placed on academic achievements. Over seventy percent of respondents agree that relevant titles should be indicated on business cards and email signatures. Additionally, Steylan Nikolov notes that *"leadership in Bulgaria has become more people-oriented, slowly turning [...] more relationship-focused"* (CCBS Survey, 2018). Bulgarians see a successful leader as someone with extensive market expertise, technical competence and organisational experience. Age and an elegant appearance are also key factors. Additionally, a leader is expected to be visionary, eloquent and a good listener (CCBS Survey, 2018).

Nearly eighty percent of the respondents agree that a leader should have high intellect, which could be linked back to their high valuation of academic achievements. Additionally, a strong charismatic personality, paired with having access to the right work networks is just as valuable. The ideology of gender equality was supported by the state during communism, which has increased the inclusion of women in the Bulgarian labour market (Bobina et al., 2017). Survey respondents largely agree that men and women have equal access to senior leadership positions, and according to the International Labour Organization, the percentage of Bulgarian women who are in senior management positions is just under forty percent (CCBS Survey, 2018; International Labour Organization (ILO), 2016).

Local leadership analysis

In-country literature review

According to Elenko Zahariev's (Еленко Захариев) *Descriptive Analysis of Corporate Culture Following the Changes*, corporate culture in Bulgaria and around the globe is filling in the gaps in economic knowledge more and more noticeably. It does so by accompanying the strategy and tactics in leadership and management (Zahariev, 2016). It can be felt in the change of manners and overall activities in various companies. These changes are, for example, an increase in compassion and tolerance, respect and responsibility.

The new corporate culture affects everyone who is part of it and demands perfecting one's leadership style (Zahariev, 2016). Business owners are no longer expected to simply assume power, administer and control, but to also lead and inspire, set up challenging goals, optimise the workflow, and keep up the optimistic mood and faith of his subordinates. Furthermore, the new generation of leaders is inclined to seek a consensus with their employees before making a decision and carefully observes and evaluates workers fairly, based on their performance (Zahariev, 2016).

Albena Taneva, PhD: a Bulgarian leadership scholar

Albena Taneva (Албена Танева) is a Bulgarian scholar and educator with a PhD in Sociology from Sofia University and extensive academic experience in the field of Leadership and Political Sciences. In addition to her work as a scholar, she has also worked for a plethora of different institutions and organisations, both governmental and in the private sector. According to Taneva (6 April 2018), the current cultural and leadership situation in Bulgaria has been heavily influenced by the political, economic and demographic turmoil, which the country has experienced in the twentieth century. Initially, in the period after the Bulgarian Liberation from the Ottoman Empire on 3 March 1878, the population was predominantly village-based. Therefore, the culture of this time period was highly collectivistic and much more egalitarian, as is expected of such communities. Thus, the Bulgarian leaders traditionally built deeper personal connections with their followers and were much more involved in their welfare (Taneva, 6 April 2018). However, with the rise of the Socialist Regime after the events on 9 September 1944, the village populations began moving towards the large cities. This trend, which Taneva (6 April 2018) refers to as *"forced urbanization"*, resulted in the formation of the political, educational and cultural elite in the country. Thus, the prevailing culture in the country became increasingly elitist, and the prevailing leadership style became highly authoritarian. Although these attitudes are still prevalent in Bulgaria today, she believes that these trends are being reversed and that the country is gradually reverting to its old identity (Taneva, 6 April 2018). When asked to describe a typical Bulgarian leader, she notes that a leader has a masculine personality with a certain level of arrogance. Based on her observations, it is crucial that the Bulgarian leader is highly communicative as she sees this as a deficit in the current cultural situation. Furthermore, a leader is expected to show determination and perseverance, even in challenging situations. With regards to differences in leadership styles between the genders, Taneva's opinion is that women tend to be more authoritarian than men (Taneva, 6 April 2018).

Borislav Ignatov, PhD: a Bulgarian cross-cultural trainer

Borislav Ignatov (Борислав Игнатов) is a Bulgarian expert and consultant on leadership and management, whose academic credentials include a Master's Degree in Business Administration from the New Bulgarian University and a PhD in Leadership from the G. S. Rakovski National Defence Academy. Furthermore, Ignatov is the Founder and CEO of Entalent Consulting, a company which focuses on corporate leadership development and management excellence.

In his experience as a leadership consultant, Ignatov has worked with a variety of Bulgarian and foreign leaders from both local and foreign companies operating in Bulgaria. *"Out of the top 100 corporations in Bulgaria, we have worked with at least half of them"* (Ignatov, 2 April 2018). Therefore, through his experience, he has accumulated a vast amount of in-depth knowledge and understanding of both foreign and local leadership styles. Ignatov (2 April 2018) describes the general Bulgarian business culture as mostly individualistic, slightly egalitarian and highly relationship-oriented. In fact, he notes that the Bulgarian business environment, as a whole, resembles a very large network of contacts and interpersonal relationships, rather than an open and highly competitive market. When asked to describe a successful Bulgarian leader, Ignatov explains: *"You should observe some of our successful political leaders. If you take a look at our Prime Minister, you will see a very common leadership style, which can be characterised as being very masculine..."* (2 April 2018). In his opinion, the typical Bulgarian leader can be characterised as exhibiting subtle arrogance, having impeccable emotional stability and exuding confidence and decisiveness, which can be seen at all times. *"In my opinion, the majority of Bulgarians would recognize such individual as a successful leader"* (Ignatov, 2 April 2018).

In-country leadership bestseller

One of the best known Bulgarian books on leadership is *Liderstvo / Лидерство* written by Dimitar Ivanov. The book notes that a major part of management in every organisation structure is the coordination of its activities and members' efforts to achieve organisational goals. This process requires the active involvement of a leader, which is an inevitable part of effective management of human capital. It becomes clear that the interpersonal relationship of leader-to-followers is closely connected with enabling the followers to perceive the group goals as their own whereby they can more easily be attained. In theory and social practice, it has been accepted that the notion of effective governance is unattainable without leadership (Ciela, 2018).

Ivanov continues with questions that have been sought by historians, pedagogues, psychologists, ethics, and other scholars in the fields of the social sciences throughout various historical eras, in the Bulgarian environment. Questions such as: can individual people be trained and questioned about leaders or are they born; why do people with different traits, education and culture manage to appear as successful leaders; is there no leadership if there are no followers (Ciela, 2018)?

Local leadership book

Title	Liderstvo / Лидерство
Author	Dimitar Ivanov
Publisher	Ciela
Year	2014
ISBN	978-954-28-1497-9

Bulgarian leadership YouTube review

In this video, Velina Getova presents her research findings, "Entrepreneurial Leaders in Quest for Authenticity and Identity Sync", at the American University in Bulgaria (AUBG), after completing her MBA at the London School of Economics. Her study showcases the definition of being a leader in the twenty-first century and how people can become better leaders. The presentation also sheds light on the Johari Window, which is a tool used by successful CEOs for self-discovery (AUBG, 2014). Getova graduated from AUBG in 2009 after which she became a consultant, career coach and entrepreneur. She founded the Center for Genuine People and Change and is currently working at PWC as a consultant (AUBG, 2014).

Getova starts by defining the 'myth of the great man' which has been covered in several theories. This great man is meant to be the great CEO, who is at the top of the hierarchy chain and is usually viewed as a great persona. A person like the great man can be considered to have superpowers, according to Getova. This is due to the fact that this person has been able to influence others and mobilize crowds to work on business challenges, which has been the method for the past decades (AUBG, 2014). In her presentation at AUBG (2014), Getova looks back at the past values of leadership when it comes to rules of success. She explains that money and power used to be the biggest factors of leadership which create a dangerous environment as it sometimes obscures the values that leaders might have. She also shares the theory of servant leadership of Robert K. Greenleaf, which is mostly about helping communities and enabling others to succeed, and not necessarily placing your own individual success as a priority. Greenleaf argues that if one wants to become a leader, it is important to learn how to serve others. A leader is not a leader if he or she does not know how to serve others (AUBG, 2014; Greenleaf Center for Servant Leadership, 2016).

Another trend that has been shared is the idea of dynamic, shared leadership which is more focused on the people and relationships instead of figures and the single great man. An example given of dynamic shared leadership is the leadership dynamics of medical trauma teams that have a common goal which does not have to be regulated by one great man: saving someone's life. These teams delegate leadership roles between each other, although it might be interfered with when the seriousness of the situation increases (AUBG, 2014). Besides dynamic leadership being visibly present in medical trauma teams, dynamic leadership also exists in start-ups. An example is co-founder teams, a group of people standing at the top, of which some more in-depth examples are fairly well-known such as Steve Jobs and Steve Wozniak. There are always at least two people, not one because leadership and entrepreneurship are more focused on teams (AUBG, 2014).

The key point of the presentation, however, is about authentic leadership - being the true version of yourself. During her research, Getova found several important items on authenticity and leadership. It is better to be a first-rate version of yourself rather than to be a copy of somebody else (AUBG, 2014).
Authentic leaders are able to show elevated levels of self-awareness and have moral values and genuine goals with which to lead the business. Money will always remain an important incentive. However, a leader should focus on creating something meaningful for the community (AUBG, 2014).
Leadership is about empathy and being supportive. When looking back into leadership in Bulgaria it also becomes clear that the principles of the past are fading as it is not about power anymore, but empowering others (AUBG, 2014).

Understanding hierarchy in Bulgaria

Traditionally, Bulgarian organisations are highly hierarchical with more layers of management than their foreign counterparts (Ignatov, 2 April 2018). Moreover, communication pertaining to decision-making between the highest and lower levels of management is insignificant. Local companies tend to exhibit a very steep pyramid-like structure, whereby decisions are taken almost entirely at the top and once made are difficult to alter (CCBS Survey, 2018).

The top of the pyramid is, of course, the leader, immediately followed by a close circle of highly trusted individuals, who are often friends or family members. According to Kicheva (2017), leaders in Bulgaria place a high priority on family, personal relationships and social groups. Unsurprisingly, this attitude is also present in the business culture, which is why it is essential to form personal connections with one's colleagues. Therefore, trust, loyalty and confidentiality are expected of Bulgarian managers and are key factors in determining their earnings and status (Ignatov, 2 April 2018).

Another key point is that social status greatly affects how individuals are perceived and evaluated by their peers and superiors. In other words, it is vital to invest time in socialising, building and maintaining relationships in order to propel oneself in the hierarchy. Katia, a Ukrainian content-manager in Bulgaria says that naming leaders by their first name *"[depends] on the relations in the company"* (CCBS Survey, 2018). Additionally, the CCBS Survey (2018) reveals that Bulgarians have a tendency to judge individuals based on attire, the car that they drive, job titles, academic achievements, charisma and soft skills.

Although the aforementioned elitist, relationship-oriented leadership style and subsequent top-down chain of command are still prevalent in the country, the opposite trend can be seen in the new generations of Bulgarian entrepreneurs (Chou, 2017). Young business leaders, who have often been educated abroad, prefer a flat hierarchy. They tend to be more individualistic and question rules and regulations (Ignatov, 2 April 2018).

How the Bulgarians achieve leadership empathy

Given the fact, that the Bulgarian culture is so strongly relationship-oriented, it should come as no surprise that empathy is an integral part of Bulgarian leadership. Having said that, it is important to understand how local leaders express empathy for their followers and use it to build and maintain good relations within their organisations.

As mentioned earlier in the chapter, it is expected of Bulgarian Leaders to display a certain degree of stoicism. According to Ivan Shopov (Иван Шопов), this emotional stability is vital for maintaining harmonious relations in the workplace because it helps to avoid impulsive, negative or aggressive behaviour and promotes mutual respect. For example, when dealing with a great deal of issues and setbacks, even otherwise psychologically stable individuals can behave irrationally or disrespectfully (Shopov, 2017). Therefore, it is imperative for leaders to remain composed and not allow frustration or fear to interfere with their interactions with their employees.

Although saving face is crucial for Bulgarian leaders, that does not mean that it is expected of them to be cold and not express any emotions. In fact, if a leader is too emotionally reserved in Bulgaria, he or she will be deemed untrustworthy (Ignatov, 2 April 2018.) However, due to the indirect communication style, which is typical for this culture, subtle out of place expressions can be misinterpreted and lead to unnecessary conflict. Hence, Bulgarian culture dictates that a leader must always be polite and respectful to the collective, while not allowing for his or her kindness to be abused (Shopov, 2017). Moreover, he or she must maintain a relaxed and optimistic mood and socialise with the group, while respecting each individual's intellect, social standing and age (Shopov, 2017). Thus, it is important to be flexible and find the right balance between formal and informal language and behaviour, while expressing his or herself clearly and rationally and communicating intentions to the point.

Lastly, it is of the utmost importance that a leader and his or her followers maintain mutual respect by showing correctness and loyalty to one another. This can be done by being punctual and supporting each other's interests (Ignatov, 2 April 2018).

Colombia

Laila Notkamp, Vincent Rosing & Jens Smit

Colombia is the only South American country with coastlines on the Pacific Ocean as well as the Caribbean Sea. The country is known for its spectacular landscapes and ecological diversity. Because of the country's wide range of altitudes, Colombia has a diversity of climates which leads to its ecological diversity.
The landscape can change within a space of a few miles from jungles to savannas, deserts, wetlands and beaches, each of which holds abundant natural resources and thousands of unique animal and plant species (Farnsworth-Alvear, Palacios & Gomez, 2016).
The gross export income originates from the coffee business. Colombia is the second biggest exporter of coffee, behind its neighbour Brazil. Other important revenue comes from the export of bananas, cotton, tobacco and cocoa.
Colombia, which is named after Christopher Columbus, is religiously dominated by the Roman Catholic community that is made up of the majority of the inhabitants. Therefore, the locals greatly respect the Catholic holidays. This results in Colombia having the most national holidays of all countries. This South American country is home to a vast and diverse population, where Spanish is the native language. Colombians originate from the Spanish, Indian and, to a lesser degree, African ancestry. Two-thirds of the people are Mestizo, which is a mixture of Europeans and Indians. Colombians of African descent and Mulattos constitute roughly to one-fifth of the inhabitants, and Caucasians amount approximately to the same number. The ethnical diversity has enriched Colombia with a broad amount of cultural expressions in art, literature and music.

How the Colombians characterise leaders

Due to the many civil wars that Colombia has battled over the years, Colombians find it hard to describe one specific type of leadership. A large number of people will declare that strict leadership, as found in an autocratic system, is the best kind of leadership. However, others will claim that leadership with empathy is even better. Nonetheless, generally speaking, the leadership style that the Colombians would most appreciate is a mix between strict and empathic leadership (Lewis, 2006).

According to Páez and Salgado (2016), the Colombian culture has three aspects that characterise the local leadership style. The culture is known for its high in-group collectivism, low institutional collectivism and high power-distance. In an interview, Professor Juan Carlos Guevara Larrahondo concludes that Colombian leaders are very autocratic. He clarifies that *"[t]here is still a strong [belief] in social status, and you can see that Hofstede's dimension of power distance in our country that is [relatively high]. So, that reflects a strong focus on status and hierarchy"* (26 April 2018).

Colombians also find status important. Professions such as doctors and teachers are often viewed with great respect (Chokar, Brodbeck & House, 2007). The results of the CCBS Survey (2018) confirm the importance of status in Colombian leadership. One respondent, Daniel, a Colombian professional in international business, explains: *"I think leadership in Colombia is about having knowledge and keeping your status quite high"* (CCBS Survey, 2018).

As a result of the high-power distance and the fact that in business status is important, there is a strict way of communicating in Colombian organisations. Just like status, hierarchy is a very important aspect of Colombian culture and results in employees being expected to accept the leadership style of their manager. There is no room for an employee to disagree with the leadership style as the employee should accept and respect the opinion of the manager. Interrupting a manager is not desirable as Lewis (2006) underlines in his work. Colombians appreciate an employee's opinion only if he or she is a specialist on a determined subject.

Survey results and what local respondents say

The survey findings below are based on opinions of local leaders and managers. While investigating local leadership characteristics, respondents describe that it is important to provide employees with a good work environment. As Alejandro Vargas, an SCM analyst puts it: *"Here it is very common to create a special environment scenery with your subordinates to make a very good relationship, and they can do their job in a good way. This scenery depends on tastes and likes that your subordinates could have"* (CCBS Survey, 2018). Consistent with Hofstede's findings, Colombia has a very dominant masculine leadership profile (Hofstede Insights, n.d.). Juan Diego Cantor agrees with Hofstede: *"In general, the vision of female leaders is less known or could have less impact in the Colombian society, because of it is male chauvinism"* (CCBS Survey, 2018).

Regarding the treatment of women in Colombian businesses, the respondents have varying perceptions. Some participants comment that due to Colombia's masculine business culture, female leaders do not have the same opportunities to grow in their role as a leader. In contrast, others will say that this is not true and that female employees have the same opportunities as men. Furthermore, to the question of whether men and women use a different leadership style, Jimena Rodriguez, an industrial engineer admits: *"Yes... Commonly we find men as a leader. But when women are the leaders sometimes [they] are more sensitive"* (CCBS Survey, 2018).

Finally, opinions about the hierarchical relations in Colombia follow. On this topic, the respondents do not agree with each other, either. Answering a question about whether Colombians value strict hierarchies or not, David, an agency coordinator, admits: *"We don't like to have in secret our criticism or opinions about the things to do better for the best teamwork"* (CCBS Survey, 2018). While another respondent, Gerald Porcario, notes that Colombia is comparatively hierarchical: *"I am [an] expat, my management style is quite far from the usual style in the country: very much hierarchy/status / top-down oriented"* (CCBS Survey, 2018).

Local leadership analysis

In-country literature review

Zárate Torres and Sergio Matviuk (2012) explain the expectations that Colombian employees have of their leaders. The two authors conducted a study to research the correlation between emotional intelligence and leadership practices with the objective to define the ideal Colombian leader. According to the article, the ideal leader is an emotionally intelligent one. This feature will also make him or her more effective and efficient than his or her colleagues (Torres & Matviuk, 2012). Additionally, the same result is repeatedly presented in the answers of the CCBS Survey (2018). About ninety percent of the respondents emphasise the importance for a manager to personally spend time on the well-being of his or her employees (CCBS Survey, 2018).

Furthermore, according to Torres and Matviuk (2012), the other main characteristics that define great leadership are to serve as an example, motivate and know how to empower to act. At the same time, a leader should not stress about sharing the vision of the organisation and does not need to challenge the process. Moreover, the encouragement to show emotions and working with them are valued highly (Torres & Matviuk, 2012).

Similar to the previously mentioned investigations, Castaño, de Luque, Wersing, Ogliastri, Fuchs, Shemueli and Robles (2015) conducted research in which respondents of various South American countries were questioned on expected leadership behaviours in their specific country. Apart from others, the participants from Colombia considered every individual that is part of a group to be responsible for the results. Thus, it will be less effective for a leader to appeal to an employee's self-interest to motivate him or her than to appeal to notions that an action is good for the group (Castaño et al., 2015). The research found that great Colombian leaders are relationship-oriented and highly value their subordinates' well-being. Leaders who do not offer this trait are perceived as "cold and lacking respect" (Castaño et al., 2015). These findings again align with the results of an investigation by Ogliastri (2012). He states three important features that an excellent leader should possess. These are managerial style, vision and human and personal relations, each of which is accompanied by discernible leadership features that are: setting objectives, taking action before a crisis and acting with integrity (Ogliastri, 2012).

Juan Carlos Guevara Larrahondo: a Colombian leadership scholar
Guevara Larrahondo (26 April 2018) states in an interview that the typical leadership style found in Colombia is "extremely autocratic." He relates this statement to Hofstede's cultural dimensions which present Colombia with a fairly high-power distance index. Furthermore, Larrahondo emphasises that the country's economy heavily depends on small- and mid-sized companies. However, *"the problem with [this] is that they do not have concrete systems to train people and to train managers in matters of leadership skills"* (Larrahondo, 26 April 2018). For this reason, leaders expect automatic respect and obedience. There is no space for open criticism towards the leader. *"Another complaint from employees is that many leaders do not know how to communicate correctly"* (Larrahondo, 26 April 2018). Yet, recently the leadership style has begun to change. Especially international or big companies initiate motivational methods, like giving the employee more freedom. This could present as giving the employee one workday per week off or allowing him or her to work from home. Guevara Larrahondo is fairly positive about the role of female leaders in Colombia. However, he adds that female leaders are currently still valued higher in international or big companies than in small Colombian ones (Larrahondo, 23 April 2018).

In-country leadership bestseller

Carlos Raul Yepes wrote the Colombian bestseller *Por otro camino: De regreso a lo humano* (On the Other Path: Back to the Human), which was published in April 2016. The author, who is the ex-president of Bancolombia, the biggest bank in Colombia, made it his mission to inspire leaders of the modern world to change their style to become more humane and make feelings an essential part of the business world. By 2011, when the author reached the presidency of Bancolombia, Yepes had faced various challenges in his life which made him want to change Bancolombia's corporate culture. Yepes created a humane culture that appreciates high ethical commitment and the feelings of its employees up to a point to where Bancolombia was called the "most humane bank". With the book, the author wants to propose a change in the business world and suggests more trust and respect within companies in order to achieve better results. Furthermore, he points out the importance of knowing oneself before judging and managing others. Moreover, he states that the essential part of being happy and content is sometimes to stop and think of oneself first.

Local leadership book		
Title	Por otro camino	
Subtitle	De regreso a lo humano	
Author	Carlos Raul Yepes	
Publisher	AGUILAR	
Year	2016	
ISBN	978-9585425033	

Colombian leadership YouTube review

The video *Fuerza en Movimiento – Liderazgo Empresarial* (Force in Motion - Business Leadership) by CNN Español (2015) investigates different Colombian leadership styles by interviewing three very successful entrepreneurial leaders. These are Oswald Loewy, president of Sempertex; Silvia Escovar, president of Terpel; and Carlos Enrique Cavelier, president of Alquería. All three are leaders of some of the currently most important and influential Colombian companies.

Loewy points out that in order to achieve the goals and missions of the company, first, the employees have to be convinced of them. Secondly, the employees have to believe in their boss, and every single part of the team has to feel important and valued. However, he also mentions that the business is not a democracy. There are ways in which employees can participate, but generally speaking, it is not possible to change the way in which the company operates. Escovar also emphasises the importance of every single part of the team feeling valued. She admits herself that she does not know everything, which is the reason why she chooses to make the entire team part of the decision-making process. Last but not least, Cavelier goes as far as expressing his resentment of hierarchies. For him, leadership needs to have a horizontal structure. He describes leadership as defining the goals of a company, not necessarily as the only leader but with the help of the entire team. On top of that, the leader should help the team to keep the objectives clear.

Understanding hierarchy in Colombia

Colombians have a strong hierarchical business structure, and it is mainly the top segment of the company that makes the decisions (Romero, 2004). Status and respect are important in a Colombian business even though it seems like a warm and friendly atmosphere. The managers demand admiration from their subordinates and are more autocratic than, for instance, Northern European managers. Professor Juan Carlos Guevara Larrahondo of the Universidad del Rosario of Bogota confirms on this matter: *"Leaders here try to be extremely bossy, autocratic. There is no openly criticizing from people under him. So, it is not common that people in companies can say what they like and what they do not like about a leader. There is too much fear."* (Larrahondo, 26 April 2018). Regarding business practices, an employee would most likely seek advice from other employees with the same status rather than ask the manager for a consult. Despite the fact that it is highly acceptable to ask the responsible supervisor for feedback, the employee's pride may stand in the way. *"That would be seen as a weakness"* (Larrahondo, 26 April 2018).

Traditionally, it is improbable to argue with someone with a higher position or giving one's opinions unless being asked for. If the manager asks for the consultation of a subordinate, it is vital that the ideas are constructed in a subtle manner. If a recommendation from a subordinate is given without it being asked for by the manager, it may seem intrusive. Normally, employees are expected to adhere to the instructions of the top segment and complete their tasks. *"It is not difficult to notice that social inequality, and the values that shore it up, is part of daily life"* (Chokar et al., 2007). The Colombian informality in social occasions may give one the impression that the companies have a less vertical structure, but the decision-making occurs in a top-down disciplined manner (Rueda Laguna, 2016)

How the Colombians achieve leadership empathy

Colombians prefer a leader who is strong and capable of making decisions. Usually, employees of this specific South American country tend to follow a charismatic leader that enforces his or her decisions. Yet, the leader should also be accessible and open for consultation. The leader is capable of seeing one's perspective on the subject. This is how the leader achieves feelings of empathy from his or her employees and business partners. The results of the study of Torres (2015), suggest that effective managers should be good problem solvers but also, be caring, considerate, participative, communicative, flexible and understanding. A good way to gain trust from colleagues is to show warmth and compassion. Achieving empathy from subordinates is mainly achieved through showing respect to the person and understanding his or her ambition.

Colombians genuinely appreciate closeness from colleagues and partners. Listening to each other's problems helps to increase the level of empathy, although it is important to let one speak at length as the Colombians can be loquacious of nature. In order to maintain the harmony in business, it is important to criticise indirectly and to give recognition regularly (Katz, 2006). Colombia's group-oriented culture is demonstrated in leadership that exalts group achievement, warm interpersonal relationships and egalitarian treatment (Badaracco & Ellsworth, 1994).

Greece

Danique Happel, Maika van der Hulst & Cees Spooren

Greece (Ελλάδα), officially called the Hellenic Republic (Ελληνική Δημοκρατία) and historically known as Hellas, is a country located in Southern Europe. The country is neighboured by Albania, Macedonia, Bulgaria and Turkey. Greece has a population of approximately 11 million people and 6 million diasporas. Most of the Greek diaspora lives in the United States, United Kingdom, Australia and Germany (De Griekse Gids, n.d.). One-fifth of Greece's land surface is made up of islands, consisting of more than 1400 island, of which Crete is the largest. Athens is the capital and the largest city on the mainland, followed by Thessaloniki (Greeka, n.d.). Greece is especially known for its history, and for ancient Greek mythology. They are the founders of the Olympics and democracy. After the Second World War, Greece rapidly changed economically and socially with tourism, imports and exports becoming major contributors to the economy (BBC News, 2018). Prokopis Paylopoulos is the president of Greece, and the head of the government is Alexis Tsipras since 18 February 2015. Their Parliament (*Vouli ton Ellinon*) has 300 seats and works with a four-year period. The motto of Greece is *"Eleftheria i Thanatos"*, which means *"Freedom or Death"*.

How the Greeks characterise leaders

In general, Greek leaders are expected to be productive and foster a proactive work environment. A leader is likely to be at the top, managing time and stress and working on the vision, plan and goals of the company. In other words, a typical leader is a charismatic person who manages to lead the business towards the desired goals and objectives (Trivellas & Reklitis, 2013). Greek leadership favours the transformational style (Avolio, Walumbwa & Weber, 2009). Transformational leadership is based on making new strategies in order to take the company towards success and to the next level of their performance. An example of how this looks in practice is given by, Panos Xenokostas, a president and CEO of a technology and system integration company: *"The first established procedure was 'how to create or change a procedure'. So, there is [a] way to adapt in business needs and at the same time able to change something that does not work"* (CCBS Survey, 2018).

Transformational leadership focuses mainly on team-building, motivation and collaboration with subordinates at different levels to accomplish change for improvements (Ingram, 2018). A leader gains respect and inspires employees, and by inspirational motivation, leaders increase understanding of shared goals, which makes it easier to bring across the high expectations of the organisation's vision. Intellectual stimulation encourages creativity and change in the employees, while, through this process, the leaders support their followers by recognising their competencies, capabilities and qualities thereby building their confidence (Simosi & Xenikou, 2010). There is some disagreement among academics and Greek professional over whether Greek leadership is typically individualistic or collectivistic. Research entitled *Cultural and Leadership Similarities and Variations in the Southern Part of the European Union*, by Nikandrou, Apospori and Papalexandris (2003), suggests that Greeks are very individualistic and independent rather than collectivistic. In the workplace it is perceived as normal for subordinates to have limitations on their freedom, independence and individual rights. Authorities are not easy to approach, as it will cause difficulties in cooperating and be interpreted as a mistrust of superiors. This individualistic leadership seems to be more prevalent in some companies than in others. Asimakopoulou stated in a recent interview on Greek leadership: *"I would say they are both, it depends on their culture and there are leaders who are individualistic and leaders who are not"* (Asimakopoulou, 15 March 2018). Family-owned businesses, for example, seem to be less individualistic.

In Greece, family businesses seem to be a new trend, in which leadership also takes another form. Many Greek managers in this field are expected to take care of their employees' needs and show interest in the problems of the company (Nikandrou, et al, 2003). The research of Nikandrou et al (2003), concludes that the Greeks value collectivism a lot and they are convinced that the power distance should be reduced. Nikandrou et al. (2003) state that family businesses are becoming popular, mainly to keep the business alive and to maintain a good relationship, the feeling as a group therefore could be essential. One of the respondents of the CCBS Survey also says *"in Greece, organisations (especially with less than 30 employees) tend to be like families"* (CCBS Survey, 2018). This idea may also be a result of how businesses are working right now as suggested by Asimakopoulou (15 March 2018), and how leaders are perceived nowadays. However, further research is required to provide support and evidence on this perspective.

Survey results and what local respondents say

The Cross-Cultural Business Skills (CCBS) Survey (2018) on Greek leadership has gathered 50 responses from local and experienced professionals who answered questions regarding their experience of leadership in Greece. Respondents vary in their opinions given as answers to the questions of some topics. First of all, to put the focus on how Greek leaders value management decisions, more than one-third of the professionals agree on the following statement: when a management decision has been made, it will not be changed easily (CCBS Survey, 2018). Similarly, for one-third of the participants missing a deadline is perceived as more or less a failure (CCBS Survey, 2018). Secondly, in terms of established procedures by employees, over half of the professionals agree that following these procedures are mandatory in Greek leadership (CCBS Survey, 2018).

The answers of our respondents about an implicit idea of how a leader ought to behave and what qualities are expected of a leader are clear. For instance, as a leader in Greece, it is important to be an intellectual, to have access to the right networks and, above all, to have a strong charismatic personality. Furthermore, employees look up to a leader on the basis of organisational experience, market expertise and technical competence. Therefore, employees expect from their leader to be a visionary thinker, a good compromiser, a good listener and most of all, a Greek leader must be a powerful decision maker.

Concerning the relationship with subordinates, over 80% of the respondents agree that a manager is expected to actively spend time on the personal well-being of the team members. According to a Greek manager in the tourist industry, *"Treating staff like family, keeps the level of respect high"* (CCBS Survey, 2018). Regarding time management, when scheduling a staff meeting, the morning is the best time according to the CCBS Survey (2018) respondents. This staff meeting is always held in the office, mostly in the meeting room.

Local leadership analysis

In-country literature review

Hierarchy is perceived as an essential part of the Greek culture. Although this is changing and the Greeks believe that they ought to be more collectivistic and have less power stratification, research conducted by Nikandrou et al (2003) indicates that many aspects of power distance can be recognised in Greece.

However, there is research that shows that Greek people valued collectivism more than any country. This statement can be supported by the number of increasing family businesses in Greece because it apparently keeps strong relationships and remains for a longer period of time (Vassiliadis & Vassiliadis, 2013). Family businesses are supported by five so-called stepping stones. The first is entrepreneurship, which is needed to transfer profession knowledge, entrepreneurial characteristics and managerial values to the next generations. The second is studies as education is seen as important in order to be able to support the business. Family members will be educated about the structures and doing business in their company to be ready when they will take over the company. It is also important for a family member to acquire outside work experience at home or abroad. Finally, one who came through all the steps will start working in the proletariat and will work their way up through every department, until they get to the highest position. This is necessary in order to gain experience in all the fields of the business and to know how they operate. Not only will they gain experience, they will also be acknowledged by their employees and are more likely to make effective and logical decisions (Vassiliadis & Vassiliadis, 2013).

A transformational leadership-style is desired in Greece as it helps the business taking steps forward through effective strategies, in order to adapt to the dynamic market and business culture (Ingram, 2018). Most businesses in Greece are result-orientated and look for achievements and actualisation of mutual desires. Organisations in Greece are perceived as having a 'constructive' cultural orientation, which means that they are more likely to induce high emotional and normative ties to their employees. According to Simosi and Xenikou (2010), these ties emphasise members' feelings of power, autonomy, self-determination as well as affiliation, which are all associated with human basic needs. Considering this information, it seems that there is a link between the relationship-based business and the transformational style of leadership that is desired.
Within the Greek culture, there is relative gender equality, and female leaders interestingly do not face significantly different attitude from subordinates and are not treated differently from male leaders. According to a satisfaction research, conducted in 1990 by Galanaki et al, subordinates in Greece do not have any preference for having either a female or male leader. In addition, they did not experience higher satisfaction with either gender. However, it does matter, if the leadership-style is totally different from what employees were hoping for (Galanaki, Papalexandris & Chalikias, 2009).

Barbara Asimakopoulou: a Greek leadership scholar

Barbara Asimakopoulou is an author and trainer for the online e-learning training program *Coaching Leadership in the Footsteps of Socrates* from the National Kapodistrian University of Athens. Aside from this, Barbara Asimakopoulou is a Greek leadership coach and founder and managing partner of Human Resources Expertise, in which she inspires and supports business owners, professionals, entrepreneurs and executives in managerial and leadership issues.

According to Asimakopoulou, leaders are respected by their subordinates, if they have great knowledge and expertise, a strong feeling for justice, responsibility, and care about the human development (Asimakopoulou, 15 March 2018). She describes good Greek leadership considering the following characteristics: empathy, inspiration, focus on positive attitude and human development.
"Empathy has to do with emotional intelligence, to understand the feelings. Talking a common language, having the same culture and educational level and to help the other part, this is empathy" (Asimakopoulou, 15 March 2018).

In-country leadership bestseller

One of the most recommended books about Greek leadership is called *Ηγεσία*. This literally translates to 'Leadership' and is written by Professor Dimitrios K. Bourantas in 2005.

Local leadership book	
Title	Ηγεσία
Subtitle	The road of lasting success
Author	Bourantas, Dimitrios K.
Publisher	Review
Year	March 2005
ISBN	978-960-218-406-6

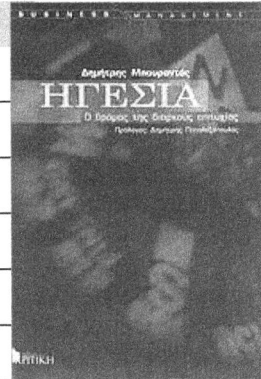

This book describes how the top companies and successful executives drive developments and ensure lasting success. In an environment that is becoming increasingly competitive, uncertain and demanding, leadership as a function of the executives of all hierarchical levels is the key to success that lasts in the long term. Bourantas (2005) decodes the 'DNA' of sustained success. This book provides a 'practical guide' on how executives can secure the strategic parameters of lasting competitiveness such as people, culture, strategies, structures, systems, constant change and adaption. The book analyses leadership roles and proposes a modern and effective model of leadership. It describes specific practices and provides useful tools, which executives are able to use to achieve outstanding performance in their organisations by inspiring, winning, and mobilising their employees. It is suggested as a necessary and useful book for all entrepreneurs as is it is a valuable tool for developing and substantially improving their way of thinking and behaviour. The book is a challenge and a driver for creating self-awareness. Additionally, it helps in creating a strong will for continuous improvement and outstanding performance and shows the way to achieve these strengths (Bourantas, 2005).

Greece leadership YouTube review

Greek people prefer personalisation of services and products. McDonald's in essence, failed in Greece when they opened their restaurants. The mistakes were found in their marketing strategy as they tried to implement it with the strategy they had executed in the United States. Panos Xenokostas says: *"Why McDonald's failed? At the same time as McDonald's started opening restaurants in Greece, another fast-food chain started opening restaurants. It was a Greek fast-food company named Goody's. As a Greek company, Goody's understands the needs of the Greek people. They personalised it. They treated their customers like they were family. Everything was personalised to the customers. So, even McDonald's who has thousands of people working and have unlimited resources, they failed because they didn't personalise".*

Greek people have respect for their boss, says Xenokostas. *"In a lot of western countries and the United States, people address their boss with Panos or John, but employers in Greece will address their bosses with Mister out of respect".* This empathises the relationship-based business style in Greece, and how important the hierarchy there is.

Leaders in Greece are characterised to be powerful decision makers. As Xenokostas states *"He rather makes a mistake, than not make a decision. Not making a decision only causes more problems. Look at our political leaders. They don't make decisions and our country is after eight years still in crisis".*

Considering doing business in Greece, Xenokostas adds *"Find the right local partner. Not a local partner, but the right local partner. Who understands the culture and understands the difference. Because, sometimes people are missing translation. It is not just speaking the right language but knowing what they say. What they really mean. In the United States if somebody says I will think about it, it is a no. If a person from Greece says I will think about it, it is a yes".* In other words, it is good to have a business partner who can be a bridge between two different cultures in order to be successful.

Understanding hierarchy in Greece

As mentioned earlier, hierarchy is considered very important in Greece. The leadership style tends to be paternalistic; leaders will consult eminent employees around them before coming to a conclusion and making a decision, but subordinates have much less responsibility and information is rarely shared. They have little influence in the decision-making process and are not usually encouraged to take responsibility in general (Nikandrou et al., 2003).

In large companies, a conventional hierarchy in the sense of clear reporting lines between superiors and subordinates is only to be found in the middle to lower levels of the organisation. 'True' hierarchies are built at the prominent level in the company on personal alliances between people in different departments of the organisation who trust and rely on each other. Family relations also play an important role and thus issues could arise for foreign managers if a family member of the company gets a senior position without any required skills or competencies (Trivellas & Reklitisb, 2013).

The younger generations do not have much influence in the business, neither have they influence in the organisation despite their higher oratory level, expertise and skills. Greeks start a relationship using job titles and their surnames. Subordinates usually address seniors in this way. The senior management is more likely to use first names among each other. Subordinates simply need to wait until they are invited to have a closer relationship with the seniors, to avoid offence. Until then, they will address the upper level with Mr, Mrs or Miss (Warburton, 2017).

Concerning gender issues in relation to leadership roles, women are rarely at the top position in Greek companies. One of the respondents on the CCBS Survey confirms that *"The men have more possibilities to have a position in the leadership team than the women"* (CCBS Survey 2018). However, women's senior positions within a business are increasing, but the masculinity in Greece makes it difficult to accept a woman to be in the controlling position (Warburton, 2017). Christos Petreas, a business, regional and tourism development management partner says *"women senior executives tend to be more demanding on their subordinates and stricter assessors of their performance"* (CCBS Survey, 2018). Because hierarchy is important in Greek organisations, it is important to make the first contact in a Greek company with the right person. To be efficient and make the most out of the business relation, getting in touch with a powerful person with enough authority is desirable. When setting up a meeting with a Greek organisation, it is essential to have a delegation of the same status as Greek people are not willing to speak or discuss with others who do not share the same rights and authority (RVO, 2017). Christos Petreas explains that *"in Greece, although western habits and managements principles are being more and more incorporated in the day-to-day management, the older 'patriarchal' style of the business leader as the 'clan leader' is still found in older enterprises. In this context the 'owner-majority shareholder-general manager' sees himself (usually it is a male dominant business leader figure) as the 'head of the business-family' and expects to be respected and listened to, as such, and that his 'commands' will be obeyed"* (CCBS Survey, 2018). As the awareness of the positions in a business are high, as read in the quote, and the top-positioned people are not willing to listen to subordinates, it is crucial to do business on the same level in Greece.

How the Greeks achieve leadership empathy

The first impression is considered an essential point in Greece when introducing one to another. A good impression includes being friendly and open while at the same time acting professionally. Empathy fully arbitrates the relationship between soft skills and the effectiveness of environmental scanning (Rahim & Marvel, 2011). As Greek people have a collectivistic feeling, one needs to blend well in the group at all times and show interest in others, to gain and remain in a good relationship. Another important aspect is that the eyes are said to be one of the most expressive parts of the body language because it is believed that strong eye contact will bring emphasis on the message the speaker wants to bring over and shows dominance and reinforces one's position as well (Lewis, 2006). Additionally, Greeks see the mastery of the Greek language as an essential part in order to obtain respect from their employees. The leader has to be a skilled orator to be able to eloquently argue and make rational conclusions and decisions. According to Asimakopoulou (15 March 2018), having a good education is not seen as important as looking at the characteristics and achieving empathy. As she suggests: *"One can empathise [with] everyone, but it is about culture. One can educate people, but it is different to give them culture, to listen actively and respectfully"* (Asimakopoulou, 15 March 2018). Understanding the culture and receiving empathy is different from having a proper education. As she describes, the most important thing about empathy is: other culture bias and listening with respect to others.

Hungary

Jeroen Dekker, Efecan Uygur & Max Veltman

Located in Central Europe, the Hungarian state was established more than a thousand years ago, making Hungary (*Magyarország* in Hungarian) one of the oldest countries in Europe. It is landlocked by seven neighbouring countries, most of which gained independence after being incorporated as a multiplicity of nationalities into the Kingdom of Hungary and the dual monarchy Austria-Hungary two centuries ago.

Hungary is one of the most linguistically and ethnically distinct countries in Europe. Hungarians share the same Uralic language family as the Finnish and Estonians, which brings us to their ethnic roots. Although classified as a Finno-Ugric people, Hungarian nationalists believe that the *Magyarok* are related to and descend from the Huns. As leader of the nationalist party, Jobbik, Gábor Vona declared: *"We are the grandchildren of Attila. We are not afraid of anyone!"* (The Orange Files, n.d.)

The *Magyar* borders have been pulsating like a heartbeat over the course of its eventful history. The present Hungary is geographically and demographically tiny compared to how it was during the Austro-Hungarian era when it was the second largest and third most populated nation in Europe. Due to war treaties, many Hungarians found themselves outside the Hungarian borders. The country housed just under ten million inhabitants in 2017 (Hungarian Central Statistical Office, 2017) while the Hungarian diaspora is made up of more than five million people (Loránd, 2017).

The Hungarian economy is mainly based on services, accounting for two-thirds of the total gross domestic product, before industry and agriculture (GDP) (Worldbank, 2016). Hungary exports more than it imports, making it one of the top 30 largest export countries in the world. Hungary has a big car industry, resulting in cars and vehicle parts as the biggest export products. The most imported goods are vehicle parts and medicinal packages. Germany is the biggest import and export partner (The Observatory of Economic Complexity, 2016).

How the Hungarians characterise leaders

The Hungarian leadership style has been influenced by its eventful history. After the Austro-Hungarian defeat in World War I and its dissolution, Hungary changed into a pseudo-fascist dictatorship; then a devastated and occupied republic led by a weak coalition; then a Communist puppet state of Stalin's empire; then a short-lived republic ferociously led by idealistic amateurs; then an intimidating and vengeful police state; then a fake socialist resort; and then, quite suddenly, a fully constitutional parliamentary democracy at the mercy of global forces (Boros-Kazai, 2005). This logically results in a prejudice that Hungarian *vezetők* (leaders) are still rather authoritarian, but there is a dichotomy in leadership characteristics. The older generation tends to be more autocratic, with a focus on the right networks and having influence. The newer generation, though, is shifting to more Westernised values, including motivating staff and ensuring good communication between leaders and subordinates (Kaposvári, 4 April 2018). Nowadays, the emphasis is put on equity, competition, achievement and success; therefore, managers in Hungary are expected to be decisive and assertive (Nedelko & Brzozowski, 2017). In a study by Anita Derecskei (2016), employees in the Hungarian labour market were asked to indicate the leadership style according to Lewin's triple classification of leadership styles. Half of them answered that a democratic leadership style applies most in Hungary; one out of five stated that an authoritarian style was more applicable.

Nevertheless, the *Journal for East European Management Studies* contradicts this prevailing democratic leadership style, stating that Hungarian managers are more likely to use their power and are more autocratic than their Western counterparts. If the managers say something, their subordinates follow. The managers have a much more powerful role with respect to telling the operators what they have to do. Of all Central Eastern European (CEE) countries, Hungarians are the ones who follow instructions the most, even if they do not agree with them. Four out of ten indicated that they obey, while only a third of Western Europeans support this statement (Borgulya & Hahn, 2008). Szalay (2002) explains that Hungarians do not openly voice their opinions and tend to assume that their leaders know best. Specifically, Hungarians are known for not speaking their minds to their leaders. Hungarian employees are more likely to indirectly disapprove of their managers and avoid confrontations. This is reflected in Hungarian proverbs; for example, they warn against voicing one's opinion: *mondj igazat, és betörik a fejed* (All truth will not bear telling) or *ne szólj szám, nem fáj fejem* (A still tongue makes a wise head) (Borgulya & Hahn, 2008). They do not say *nem* (no) but could sabotage what they do not concur with. Kaposvari (4 April 2018) observes the same: *"Towards the boss you say yes, yet you come out and start talking with others a lot. But you learn face-to-face to the boss to say yes."* Borgulya and Hahn (2008) also provide a cause for this attitude. They state that it is still common for Hungarian leaders to share very little or only selected information with their employees. This means that the employees have reason to believe that their boss is able to assess situations better because he or she has more knowledge of the circumstances.

Survey results and what local respondents say

Over more than fifty CEOs, managers, and leaders have answered the survey and given their opinion on and experiences with leadership in Hungary. The Hungarian leaders are not unanimous about a specific leadership style, which can be concluded from the answers of the survey, as these are much divided. When asked on what basis subordinates look up to their leaders, the majority answers that organisational experience, technical competence and market expertise are most important. These factors are more crucial than, for instance, respectable age or family background (CCBS Survey, 2018). Since the new (millennial) style of leadership in Hungary, the importance of steep hierarchy in companies has reduced, which became clear by the answer of over eighty percent of the respondents, who are now able to address their leader by the first name. But Kaposvári points out: *"Addressing by the first name only in words, not in written communication or not in front of outsiders"* (CCBS Survey, 2018). Also, a result of the change in style is evident in the fact that over three-quarters of the managers mentioned that their employees appreciate having personal contact and seeing that their leaders show an interest in their personal well-being. This is also the way a leader could generate empathy and refers to the new egalitarian atmosphere. Arising from the transition is the emerging position of women in leadership functions. Due to the Soviet regime, the number of women in charge is relatively low. A few reasons for this are given by the respondents. *"Women try to adapt to masculine style leadership in order to succeed and overwork"* is an often-named answer. *"Women are heavy-handed and very competitive, which is similar to men"* (CCBS Survey, 2018). This is confirmed by Anna Kaposvári: *"The imprint of the Soviet regime is still there. People do not come up with their own opinion, they look for a higher ranked person and try to follow him and probably not her. In leadership, women are underrepresented..."* (CCBS Survey, 2018).

The Soviet regime has also left an imprint on the decision-making process in Hungarian organisations. Three-quarters of the respondents indicate that management makes the decisions and that this will not change easily. Just like this manager opines: *"Everyone may give their opinion, but I will make the final call"* (CCBS Survey, 2018). Thus, there is some space for feedback, but the decisions will be made by the *Ügyvezető* (manager) or *Igazgató* (Director). Managers like to have some competition between the team members to gain better results, but this will not affect the manager's point of view.

Local leadership analysis

In-country literature review

In the *Debreceni Műszaki Közlemények*, the journal of the Faculty of Engineering of the Debrecen University, Dobi, Szücs, Takács and Matkó (2013) write about the relationship between leadership and organisational culture. Dobi et al. (2013) conclude that there is a difference in leadership styles within different parts of Hungary. In Debrecen, Hungary's second largest city, the style contrasts with the capital Budapest as with Nyíregyháza, a smaller city in the east of Hungary. They found that Debrecen companies are distinguished by self-consciousness and strong regulation in leadership, which is why prestige, hierarchy, and conflict resolution are important here. The organisational culture in this city is characterised by a task-oriented culture, where tasks have to be performed very precisely. The subordinates are transformed and broken down into each project and work.

Secondly, in Budapest, a strong leadership style is preferred. Organisations in Budapest are characterized by a power culture. In this culture, it is very important that leadership is centred. Furthermore, it is essential that the values of the leaders include encouragement and a preference for social relationships because they believe in an individual and the development of the individual. Thirdly, in Nyíregyháza, the organisation is characterised by role culture. Here, safety and the precise performance of tasks are typical. It may be stated that leadership and organisational culture cannot be separated. Management affects organisational culture, and elements of organisational culture have implications for leadership (Dobi et al., 2013).

Tamas Banki, a Hungarian professional, makes the same distinction between the different parts of Hungary. He says that the leaders can be divided into four groups: an older generation in the cities, an older generation in the countryside, the millennial generation in the cities, and the millennial generation in the countryside. Banki indicates that *"these four groups communicate [and] lead in a very different way. [Additionally] there are the multinational corporation leaders, who are a whole different case"* (CCBS Survey, 2017).

Anna Kaposvári and Zoltan Buzady: Hungarian leadership scholars

In order to broaden the view on Hungarian leadership, two scholars were interviewed. Anna Kaposvári is a talent and career manager at the Central European University in Budapest. In this function, she liaises with many Hungarian companies. The second interviewee is Dr Zoltan Buzady, who holds a PhD in strategic management. He has been working with leadership concepts for 25 years, in both theory and in practice. The topics concern Hungary-specific leadership traits, the implications of the past and the future of Hungarian leadership.

To begin, both scholars touch upon the split in leadership styles between the past and the present. They refer to this style as socialistic or communistic, with leaders characterised such as the *"command and control type, having little democratic processes and little understanding of humans"* (Buzady, 6 April 2018). Hungarian leaders nowadays are more open and communicative and understand their subordinates and their lives. In order to be a good leader, one does not need to have the right connections or influential family but needs to have a *"proven track record"* (Buzady, 6 April 2018; Kaposvári, 4 April 2018).

Continuing, Buzady elaborates on the principles he teaches at various business schools in Hungary, reflecting that these do not vary from neighbouring countries: *"basically anyone coming to Hungary is learning automatically through the basic similar topics like how to build up trust, how to motivate people and how to manage power in a productive way"* (6 April 2018). There is, however, a distinctive difference in managing employees in Hungary, argues Buzady, because it takes more time for Hungarian managers to build up trust than it does for managers in Western countries. This is because Hungarian subordinates first have to feel how the leaders act. For instance, is he or she inclined to be opportunistic? Therefore, respect and trust can be gained by proving your expertise, delivering on the promises you make, being professional or doing certain activities that are relevant to the team (Buzady, 6 April 2018).

Additionally, Kaposvári explains what she calls *"the land of the 'forward managers', because everybody is always forwarding via email the problem we have to solve"* (4 April 2018). In Hungary, leaders tend to have problems with taking responsibility and are likely to delegate as much as they can. Buzady (6

April 2018) acknowledges this: *"it becomes a common theme here in Hungary that we like to postpone decisions."*
Buzady then explains that the Hungarian managers nowadays struggle with attracting and retaining employees. Generally, they still have the old logic where salaries and bonuses were the biggest motivators for employees. However, nowadays managers believe that, instead of telling employees what they can earn, they also need to enjoy their work and be able to grow the skill used in their job. Buzady elaborates: *"[When the employee] becomes an expert in whatever their work is, maybe very simple to very complex, this is a much better way to motivate than to motivate them through wages"* (6 April 2018). He explains that this phenomenon is a core concept of positive psychology and is coined as "Being in Flow". It is defined as the 'optimal experience' during any activity, including your professional work, when you lose yourself in the work with time elapsing fast, which as a result leaves you with the feeling that you had a good, enjoyable working day. This Flow is nowadays implemented in leadership education so as to create a Flow-promoting work environment in which subordinates can reach this Flow mental-state (Buzady, 6 April 2018).

Dániel Gergely Szabó: a Hungarian cross-cultural trainer
Dr Dániel Szabó, who holds a PhD in Law, is an intercultural trainer and a Hungary country specialist at C3 Consulting. Currently active in the United States, he has years of knowledge and experience in leadership and in his function as a consultant and trainer. The Skype interview (6 April 2018) with Dr Szabó mainly comprised the topic of the leadership style transition visible in Hungary. Szabó starts off with the general leadership characteristic style visible in Hungary.
He admits that: *"The older archetype is definitely authoritarian because the society is very hierarchical",* linking this to the Communist times of Hungary, but follows up on the transition by mentioning that *"you also see more modern, more Western-European leaders in Hungary"* (6 April 2018). Szabó associates the modern style with new innovative and entrepreneurial businesses, and in his own experience to businesses with younger and more diverse people.
When asked about Hungarian mentality and behaviour in the working environment, Szabó replies: *"Hungarians tend to be more reserved, more self-controlled."* They do not openly oppose because generally there is a high Power Distance between subordinates and leaders. Hungarians are accepting of the power distance but can undermine leadership behind their backs if they do not agree with decisions or share the same opinions, in which case they may *"openly agree with the leader but then do things their own way"* (6 April 2018).

He continues: *"This would be less of an issue in a modern style company, but still not as likely as in the Western-European setting"* (6 April 2018)
Continuing on how leaders achieve empathy in Hungary, Szabó mentions that in an older style company, you have to be a knowledgeable professional in that company's area of work, having an answer to all work-related questions. He clarifies: *"For example, if you want to be a leader in engineering, you have to (or it is better to) be an engineer yourself"*. Seniority also plays a big role, as Szabó predicates: *"Hungarians appreciate older leaders more"*. He adds that the same goes for younger companies but to a lesser extent, where younger leaders are increasingly more of a common sight (Szabó, 6 April 2018).

In-country leadership bestseller

Verzetés- és szervezetpszichológia (Management and Organization Psychology) is a bestseller about Hungarian leadership that is written by Sándor Klein. First published in 2001, it has been republished multiple times. The goal of the book is to provide a textbook about psychology on local leadership that is understandable for everyone. The easy way of explaining is one of the factors which makes this book a bestseller. The book is used by many psychology students at Hungarian universities. The following topics are covered in the book: planning and organisation, persuasion and pursuit of quality.

Local leadership book	
Title	Vezetés- és szervezetpszichológia
Subtitle	-
Author	Sándor Klein
Publisher	EDGE 2000 KFT
Year	2001
ISBN	978-963-976-0387

Hungarian leadership YouTube review

This paragraph will discuss short interviews held by the Hungarian department of Krauthammer, which offers consultancy services in a wide range of countries. In these YouTube interviews, each interviewee discusses the state of leadership in Hungary and the way that they work as leaders of different companies.

Firstly, Zsolt Bella, working for BT Hungary, points out that a good leader *"can create a learning and sharing environment because basically what's happening is, we have many new joiners [...] that really need to get involved in what we do [...] to ensure that the team is really working within the best quality"* (Krauthammer Magyarország, 2015). He also emphasises the importance of motivation and that there has been a shift, between the past and now, in the way leaders motivate their staff: *"[...] you had your tasks, you had your to-dos, you just [did] it and that was it. But now I think that people are looking for a little more than that, as this is a big part of their life [...] [it is] important that they also have fun"* (Krauthammer Magyarország, 2015).

Secondly, Berta Csonka, president of EB OVO, clarifies her behaviour as a leader in Hungary: *"I am the katalysator [catalyst] of EB OVO, the person who is encouraging people in this group to work, and I am trying to figure out the right direction. The leadership I have to keep in mind is to constantly improve and being exemplary"* (Krauthammer Magyarország, 2015). Next to her behaviour, Csonka elaborates on the personal aspect of leading in Hungary: *"I have to be interested in my team and my team members, that is most important and one of the most difficult."* The third point she explains is: *"if someone is open and communicative, it is easy to be understood. Then it is better to restructure your personal goals"* (Krauthammer Magyarország, 2015). The last interviewee is the CEO Automotive Products at BOS Hungary, Gerhard Fischbach. Fischbach accentuates the leadership style necessary for the future: *"Only a cooperative leadership style can handle such complex problems"* (Krauthammer Magyarország, 2015). He believes that *"the average autocratic leadership style you can find in many countries, even in Hungary, will not solve the problems as it is needed for future challenges"* (Krauthammer Magyarország, 2015).

Understanding hierarchy in Hungary

Hierarchy in Hungary can be defined in two ways: an older, conservative approach and a newer, modern one. As stated by a Hungarian professional: *"I think there are two types of leadership styles in Hungary. The old-fashioned way and the new way. In the old-fashioned way, the leaders stand above the workers and the leaders will make the decisions. In the new way, people are more on one level"* (CCBS Survey, 2017). Another professional from the CCBS Survey (2016) confirms that: *"In contrast to the old, masculine, autocratic style, a modern, agile and human oriented style is characteristic of start-ups and smaller entrepreneurial companies."*

When looking at the Power Distance Index of Hofstede Insights, it is seen that Hungary scores low on a global level and average on a European level. This indicates that Hungarian individuals are less accepting of authority, have equal rights, superiors are accessible, they rely on team members to a certain degree and the attitude towards managers is informal (Hofstede Insights, n.d.). What can be deduced from this is that especially later generations are less accepting of authority while older generations and traditional businesses still rely on it. As one professional from such a traditional business puts it: *"There is great respect for the leader, management decisions are executed without discussion"* (CCBS Survey, 2016). Attitude towards managers is also an interesting subject to follow up on. As an example, the way managers are addressed is less formal among the new generation, and one manager explains that *"I personally do not care how my employees address me, as long as they feel comfortable with it. Respect does not come with a title"* (CCBS Survey, 2017). This is in contrast to the traditional companies mentioned above, as another professional answers: the question whether employees can address their leaders by the first name: *"In some traditional companies, this is not true. There, Mr Director is considered as a norm"* (CCBS Survey, 2016).

The difference that exists between these two mindsets is best described by Smith, Dugan and Trompenaars (1996) as the conservatism versus egalitarian commitment. Hungary, being an ex-communist country, has felt the impact of communism, in which obedience to the party and its ideology was the governing management philosophy, which gave a certain distinctive character to the organisations and managers operating within that system (Suutari & Riusula, 2001). *"The effects of this still exist in the Hungarian working atmosphere but historically, on the other hand, [...] Hungary have their roots in the same individualistic traditions as Western Europe and the USA, and it is thus natural that the level of individualism has increased after the collapse of communism"* (Suutari & Riusula, 2001, p. 15). This shifted the hierarchical system of Hungary from highly autocratic to a more progressive and egalitarian state of mind nowadays.

How Hungarians achieve leadership empathy

In terms of empathy for leaders, it is necessary to keep in mind that "[w]ork-related values represent an art of people's value scale that constitutes the basis for their everyday behaviour, decisions and interactions" (Borgulya & Hahn, 2008). Hungarians are very close to each other. They frequently have physical contact. If there is a meeting, shaking hands is mandatory. Often, Hungarian families live in one house, and they are very social with each other. This shows that personal contact means a lot to them. Because Hungarians are social, they really appreciate it when the boss takes them to a local restaurant or café. The socialising is especially important (Lewis, 2005). Hungarian managers often pay attention to things such as family matters and the birthdays of their subordinates, which indicates that traditions which were part of the culture under communism still exist to some extent (Suutari & Riusula, 2001, p. 25). But in reality, this disappoints: *"on weekends going with your fellow colleagues to a garden party or something like that doesn't happen too often. The people have their friends outside of the company"* (Kaposvari, 4 April 2018).

The Hungarians respect the intelligence of a leader. They respect the intelligence as is presented by academic records and by intelligent conversations, particularly about history. For a Hungarian, the history of the country is very important. As a leader, you need to know this history to some extent and anticipate on it. The results from the CCBS Survey also confirm that intelligence is highly valued. Additionally, a leader must be a charismatic person and have the right network (CCBS Survey, 2018). Buzady agrees: *"The Hungarian managers will not be accepted immediately. They have to be an expert in the field and have a good track record. This takes many years"* (Buzady, 6 April 2018). The leader also must show his or her status. Hence the Hungarians are impressed by the wealth of a leader. A leader should have a luxurious office, car and house. There are also accepted ways for a leader to present him or herself, such as wearing classy clothing and demonstrating energy and a sharp wit. Otherwise, the level of empathy is less, and your employees will work less hard.

India

Wiebe de Boer, Bob Kleingeld & Mahesh Vasnani

India is a country known for its rich diversity, ranging from its variations in languages and dialects to the contrasts in the local flora and fauna. Due to the immense size of India, local culture can differ greatly from region to region, making it possible for two individuals born and raised in India to feel a complete disconnect with one another. These factors make communication in the Indian business environment more challenging than in countries with a more uniform culture and language. From an international business perspective, India appears to be an ideal place to do business; a vast population speaks English and also has more and more spending power. India is home to modern industries, such as IT and Business Process Outsourcing, and the universities have future-based outlook (Zubko & Sahay, 2010).

However, appearances can be deceiving. For instance, international business can be slowed down by the country's corrupt and bureaucratic tendencies. Although the English language is widely used in business, language in India is much more complicated. The level of spoken English can vary considerably from person to person. Twenty-two different languages are recognised as official within the Indian constitution (Ministry of Law and Justice, 2016). This ensures that communication can be more arduous than previously anticipated.

As the second largest country in the world, following China, the size of the population has been estimated to grow at a heightened pace. The United Nations has projected that India will surpass China as the most populous country in the world (United Nations, 2017). India's GDP has been growing rapidly for the last few decades, and the growth is expected to remain solid now that the Indian government has been working on opening up to international businesses (World Bank, n.d.). Despite it taking time and effort to understand Indian culture, the country offers great potential for every foreign business that wants to go into one of the largest economies and countries in the world. The pivotal knowledge given in this chapter can help managers and businesses gain that competitive edge in India.

How the Indians characterise leaders

In India, there is not one specific leadership style that is considered to be dominant. The sharp cultural contrasts make it increasingly hard for managers to use a one-size-fits-all strategy that works the best for every Indian and company. In India, there is a big focus on transformational leadership. This occurs, according to Burns (1978), when a leader *"engages with others in such a way that the leaders and followers raise one another to higher levels of motivation and morality"* (p. 20).

According to Chokar, Brodbeck and House (2007), effective leaders in India are greatly focussed on the team, where the manager is the leader and should inspire the team and concern himself or herself with the tasks at hand. Focus group studies, done by the aforementioned authors, show that great emphasis is given to the capabilities of managers to use and communicate their vision (Chokar et al., 2007). A large majority of CCBS Survey respondents acknowledges this statement. An Indian leader is expected to be a visionary thinker and use his or her charismatic personality to ensure dedication and commitment to the company goals (CCBS Survey, 2018). According to Naresh Khatari (2005), a combination of vision and charisma is needed for successful business in India: *"charismatic leaders with no vision can also be ineffective"* (p. 23). Khatari then refers to Indira Gandhi as an example of a beloved charismatic leader who came under fire for lack of vision for the country, together with trying to gain more power for herself. This lack of leading by example through vision, lead to Indira's reputation of a dictator (Khatari, 2005).

Furthermore, leaders in India focus more on empowering their employees, than traditional Western companies. Role models and teachers are seen as guides and a source of empowerment (Cappelli, Singh, Singh & Useem, 2010). This finding is consistent with the results of the CCBS leadership survey, where a vast majority of the respondents reported to look up to their leader on the basis of them being a powerful decision maker. Moreover, respondents show that once a management decision is made it takes a lot of effort to change it (CCBS Survey, 2018). This shows that people in India trust, to a great extent, in their leaders to make the right decision. Employees in India will still look for guidance and assistance from their leader, even if they are capable to do the task by themselves (Sinha, 2008). As one Managing Director in the Indian Financial services sector concludes: *"Generally, employees expect the leader to know all the answers that they don't know"* (CCBS Survey, 2018).

However, a team focus and vision is not enough for an Indian leader to be successful. The CCBS Survey (2018) has shown that the most important trait for a leader to have is intellect. Having the best education available is fundamental in India. It is seen by many as the greatest investment (Kumar & Sethi, 2005). For this reason, it can be valuable for foreigners to list educational degrees from respectable institutions on their business cards.

To conclude, a leader should have strong listening skills, understand human aspirations and possess an emotional aspect to his or her personality that might turn employees into followers. The basic qualification of a leader is someone who touches the sentiments of an employee and has an impact on the employee to build commitment and drive.

Survey results and what local respondents say

When focussing on time management in India, from an outsider's point of view, it can appear as if Indians do not care about deadlines. However, the opposite is true. When discussing deadlines with Indians, it is important to know that the Indian side will rarely say 'no' (Millar, 2008). That is because people in India are very proud and do not want to lose face. Thus, often the Indian party will say 'yes' to a deadline, even when the group knows that they will not be able to make the deadline. This can create confusion and conflict between both sides of the conversation.

Regarding meetings, the results of the CCBS Survey show that more than seventy percent of the respondents prefer having staff meetings in the office before lunch. Thirty-three percent indicates that the ideal time for staff meetings is between 10 am and 11 am (CCBS Survey, 2018).

When discussing women in leadership roles, the CCBS Survey shows that only 22 percent of the respondents disagree with the statement that women have equal access to senior leadership positions. Indian women have had a significant role in Indian culture, for instance, Indira Gandhi who was voted as the first female prime minister of India in 1967. Women in India have, like in many countries, a dominant leadership role in family life. One male respondent mentioned: *"As a mother is first a teacher, I would see this leadership skill in a lady boss with respect and seek what I will learn new in correcting myself for improvement"* (CCBS Survey, 2018). A copious number of respondents mention that leadership qualities cannot be assigned solely on the basis of gender and indicate that the focus should be on the individual's qualities. However, female leaders were called more *"meticulous"* and *"more hands-on"* (CCBS Survey, 2018).

Ellina Rath, an Indian brand associate for the global advertising agency Leo Burnett, notes: *"I think Indian women are much more versatile than their male counterparts. Women who are at the helm truly are all-rounders in a way"* (CCBS Survey, 2018).

Honorifics, or addressing someone in the correct manner, is essential in Indian business culture. Using the appropriate title shows that the right amount of respect is given. For older or more senior leaders, this is of higher importance than for younger colleagues or subordinates. Indians give extra honour and recognition to their elders and more senior leaders. Hence, it is generally expected that those senior or older leaders are addressed by their last name as well their respective titles. Chokar, Brodbeck and House (2007) assert that: *"Honorifics such as Mr., Mrs., Sir and Madam, and their equivalents in Indian languages are widely used"* (p. 992). Similarly, the usage of the right business title can help a foreigner navigate easily through their business dealings. The common use of English titles in Indian companies simplifies this for foreigners who are able to communicate in English. In the CCBS Survey (2018) participants were asked to mention the most used leadership titles. The results show that CEO and Managing Director are the most commonly used titles.

Local leadership analysis

In-country literature review

With India's variegated cultures it is no surprise that there is more than one leadership style identifiable in the country. In their research on how Indian leaders impact employee creativity, Gupta and Singh (2012) found that leading by example and task-oriented behaviour are very important in Indian business culture. They argue that leaders could enhance employee involvement by checking up and correcting them throughout the process (Gupta & Singh, 2012). In 1984, Professor Sinha noted that, *"An ideal superior is not just a boss whose authority is delimited by the organizational manual or task requirements: he represents a benevolent source on which subordinates can depend for indulgence"* (Sinha, 1984, p. 86).

Transformational leadership is very common in India and research has shown that this style has positive merits when adopted in India. S. Pradhan and R.K. Pradhan (2015), in their investigation on the effects of transformational leadership, conclude that: *"an employee who perceives his/her immediate supervisor as transformational will tend to be more committed towards the organization and will also display extra-role behaviours that are not the explicit part of their job roles"* (p. 233).

Prof Devesh Sood: an Indian leadership scholar

Senior Professor of Indian Culture and History, Devesh Sood, was interviewed to gain insights on leadership in India. Being a renowned researcher in the state of Rajasthan, North-western India, he has written several books on Indian culture that were published by top publishers in India. According to Sood, a person in India is perceived as a leader when having certain qualities that can be found in ancient stories or wisdom. Prof Sood notes that *"A lot of subordinates look [for] characteristics of Lord Rama in their leaders"* (Sood, 18 March 2018). These include having a strong personality, being outspoken and being the type of leader who carries the whole team along with him or her. Admiration on a personal level and the ability to influence people is also highly valued. As an example, Sood (18 March 2018) mentions Ratan Tata, a leader of TATA group conglomerate. He applauds his leadership style, as it helped sustain the growth of TATA group for several decades. Furthermore, Sood notes that in order to establish a relationship with his or her subordinates, a leader should communicate with the team on a personal level. He or she needs to understand the needs and aspirations of the people that he or she is leading and be capable to help fulfil them. That is the moment when people start to build genuine trust and a relationship. Moreover, the Indian leadership style is mostly authoritarian which means that the leader with the highest authority makes decisions (Sood, 18 March 2018). This complements the data found in the CCBS Survey (2018), that employees look for their leader to make decisions.

Vinayak Pandey: an Indian cross-cultural trainer

Vinayak Pandey, Vice President of the company Pd Cor Consultancy, shared his views and opinions during an interview regarding leadership in India. He is currently involved in infrastructure projects that involve the government as well as local- and multinational companies such as the Tata Group.
First of all, Pandey (16 March 2018) explains that leadership starts by leading yourself and then others. He defines leadership as a person's ability to successfully deal with aspects which are not under his or her direct control or influence. In order to create a bond with employees, a leader has to identify individual motivation. However, there is not one set of tactics that work for every individual, each person requires a different approach. Therefore, a leader's job is to smartly develop different approaches and motivational factors.

Secondly, Pandey (16 March 2018) mentions that Indians are far more confident now, than they were some time ago and see they themselves as second to none. They perceive themselves to be on equal ground with key players in the global business environment. It is important for entities, especially traditional key-players, to realise this and not talk down or immediately assume that they are the dominating party. Thirdly, the way of giving feedback in India relates to what Pandey claimed before as being the one-on-one relationship of the leader and employee. Every individual requires a different approach: direct or indirect. In addition, Pandey asserts that all employees are involved in the decision-making process of a company (18 March 2018). Finally, Pandey points out that he does not believe in a particular method or process that everyone should follow. In his opinion, it is more about the personality aspect. Within the same working environment, different approaches are needed for different personalities. This does not tend to create complications because he perceives Indians as very open, liberal and argumentative. It is common that Indians want to debate their viewpoint with counter viewpoints (Pandey, 18 March 2018).

In-country leadership bestseller
In 1999, Robin Sharma wrote the business fable *The Monk who Sold his Ferrari,* a fictionalized tale about his own experiences of leaving a top tier job at the age of 25 to become a monk (Robin Sharma, n.d.). In 2003, Sharma published the follow-up book *Leadership Wisdom: from the Monk Who Sold His Ferrari*, where he introduces eight leadership lessons everyone ought to learn.

Local leadership book		
Title	Leadership Wisdom From the Monk Who Sold His Ferrari	OVER ONE MILLION COPIES SOLD
Subtitle	The 8 rituals of visionary leaders	ROBIN SHARMA
Author	Robin Sharma	LEADERSHIP WISDOM FROM THE MONK WHO SOLD HIS FERRARI
Publisher	Jaico Publishing House	
Year	2003	
ISBN	978-8179922316	THE 8 RITUALS OF VISIONARY LEADERS

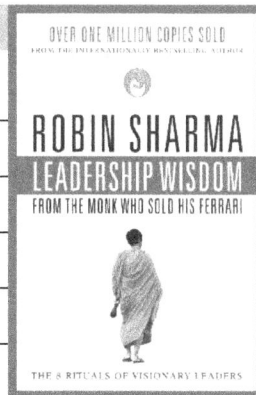

Following his success as an author, Sharma has become one of the world's leading experts on leadership and is a sought after as a keynote speaker and trainer. What makes the book interesting is that it combines current business tips together with old ritualistic wisdom (Robin Sharma, n.d.). This makes it excellent for managers who want to learn more about leadership in India as leadership and culture in India are heavily influenced by ancient religion, traditions and wisdom. Plus, the use of a fictionalised story makes it an easy read.

Indian leadership YouTube review

Leadership has been prevalent in India since ancient times. It started with a Hindu epic called *Mahabharata*. In this tale, the first leadership traits were recognised and observed. According to Dr Tejinder Sharma (2017), there are several types of leadership styles used in India. Those are: authoritarian, participative, free-rein, bureaucratic, manipulative and expert leadership. These leadership styles are adopted by organisations and incorporated into their structure. The authoritarian leadership style is practised most in organizations. This means that subordinates are closely supervised by their leaders and do not participate in the decision-making process (Sharma, 2017). Authoritarian leadership also takes place in traditional family-owned businesses. The rules and regulations do not influence the decision-making process at top level management. The top positions in the company are always inherited by family members without consideration of the subordinates. Authority is generally not delegated. In bureaucratic organisations, common in India, especially in businesses connected to the government, a bureaucratic style is used. Decisions are made with the help of superiors, but they have to comply with all the strict rules and regulations. The consequences are status differentials, slow decision making and implementation and impersonal relationships (Sharma, 2017).

Understanding hierarchy in India

Hierarchy is very apparent in India. The lines of authority in large businesses are very clear and recognising the correct social status can make or break business deals. On Hofstede's Power Distance scale India scores a high 77 out of 100, which shows that there is *"an appreciation for hierarchy and a top-down structure in society and organizations"* (Hofstede Insights, n.d.). The basis for this can be found in India's rich history: for the longest time the caste system separated Indian society into four groups, and these groups rarely mixed.

The caste system was based on ancient Hindi scripture, although it influences hierarchy, any deriving discrimination based on it is illegal (Zubko & Sahay, 2010). Furthermore, the caste system can also be used to explain, for some part, that within the business culture status is very important. For instance, it is customary for managers to get the better and larger offices and other benefits that distance them from other lower level personnel (CCBS Survey, 2018). The statistics of our leadership survey show that the majority of Indian leaders do not like to be given negative feedback during meetings. They prefer to receive it afterwards (CCBS Survey, 2018). This finding reinforces Hofstede Insights' (n.d.) assertion that: *"Communication is top down and directive in its style and often feedback which is negative is never offered up the ladder"*. Other aspects that managers should look out for is to not cross the existing lines of power, especially when employees can see it because it is seen as diluting the authority of the executive or CEO (Zubko & Sahay, 2010). Sood (18 March 2018) admits that hierarchy is still very prevalent in India as the relationship between boss and subordinate is quite distant. For instance, leaders do not often welcome the suggestions and ideas of their subordinates. These are all examples that show the clear lines of authority in Indian business. But this is not the only hierarchical model in India. According to Zubko and Sahay (2010), there is also a more flexible hierarchical model; *"This integrative model recognizes leaders within the team in different capacities, rather than above them"* (p. 66). The authors argue that a more integrative model is up and coming as an alternative to the more traditional hierarchical model. In this view, team members are not just individual contributors to a team or task but are seen more as part of the whole process. This increases the importance of the employee, rather than just the leader. This style will lead to more personal commitment to a team and eventually its goal (Zubko & Sahay, 2010). To conclude, hierarchy in India is more complicated than it appears. From a historical perspective, the harsh lines between authority come from the country's religious background. This is still evident in most companies, but in a more integrative way, with softer lines of authority.

How Indians achieve leadership empathy

In India, empathy is considered as an important skill to maintain professional success. This means that the leader understands the parties around him or her well and vice versa. Research has shown that more than 80 percent of the respondents tend to care about the wellbeing of their employees (CCBS Survey, 2018). This allows them to gain valuable information on the perspective of their employees, which can help improve the business and its strategy. Our data also shows that Indian employees look for a manager or a leader who is a good listener. This listening skill can help them gain that aforementioned information and perspective (CCBS Survey, 2018).

According to Lewis (2006), empathy in India is generally achieved through warmth, respect and properness. In addition, he states that it is important to show empathy to people when they face complications. One of the key motivations on how Indians achieve leadership empathy is by being sensitive and understanding to the people around them. India tends to be a bureaucratic country, and in order to be able to work with Indian leaders, one has to learn how to cope with the restrictions that arise from this (Lewis, 2006). Meanwhile, Sood (18 March 2018) notes that leaders are "*generally considerate*". This is in compliance with the CCBS Survey (2018), which shows that the responding leaders say that they think about the happiness of their employees. Sood (18 March 2018) also mentions that in India good examples of motivational factors are: personal appreciation, recognition and a proper and healthy working environment. He also mentions that Indians are really sentimental and emotional. Therefore, one should refrain from talking in a negative manner about religion and culture, or show any negative emotions (Sood, 18 March 2018). In keeping with this, Vinayak Pandey asserts that leadership empathy is about human understanding. By this, he means that leaders should have a humane touch and be able to identify and engage in the situation of the individual (Pandey, 16 March 2018).

Finally, it is common in India to be open to more than one interpretation and to be able to look at things from another perspective (Lewis, 2006). Supporting people's involvement helps create a pleasant working environment. It requires a strong relationship between the leader and his or her employees. For this, the leader has to truly make an effort in understanding his or her employees and give a genuine recognition and take a personal interest. Sood emphasises that a leader should communicate with the team on a personal level. It has to become a daily effort instead of a selective one (Sood, 18 March 2018).

Kazakhstan

Thomas van Cappellen, Raymon Foget & Joost van Vliet

Kazakhstan (Қазақстан) is the ninth largest country in the world. Kazakh means *"wanderer"* and stan means *"land"*, therefore Kazakhstan is also known as *"Land of the wanderers"*. It is located in Central Asia and surrounded by Russia, China, Kyrgyzstan, Turkmenistan and Uzbekistan. The country is sparsely populated with almost twenty million habitants living in a large territory but has more than a hundred nationalities. About three million of them live in the two largest cities: Almaty and the capital Astana. Astana literally means *"capital city"*, but it has only been the capital city of Kazakhstan since 1997. In general, the people who live in these cities are the most prosperous of the country.
The native language in Kazakhstan is Kazakh, but the influence of the Soviet Union on the language is still detectable. Under Soviet rule, the Kazakh language was oppressed which has resulted in a Russian business language (GOV UK, n.d.). After the Soviet Union collapsed in the early nineties, Kazakhstan became an independent country. Independence had significant consequences for the economic activities. A few years after independence, the local economy was strengthened by the exportation of energy and mineral sources (Bendini, 2013). Due to the strong economic development, the government started to improve the infrastructure to attract more international companies and develop the tourism.

How the Kazakhstani characterise leaders

In general, the Kazakhstani leadership style can be characterised as relationship-oriented. Adriaan Meijer (13 March 2018), one of the directors at Air Astana, explains this in an interview *"A Kazakh leader has to show to his people that he is aware of the task that has to be done and that he cares for his people"*. Increasingly, Kazakh leaders are becoming more independent, and make all the decisions themselves (Hofstede, n.d.). Moreover, results from the GLOBE project, which visualises leadership characteristics of different countries across the world, show that Kazakh leaders have the ability to set up a team and communicate effectively with other members, but they have a strong interest in protecting their own position as a leader (Gupta, Hanges & Dorfman, 2002). The real goal of teamwork, according to the CCBS Survey (2018), is not to achieve the best performance for the company: *"Usually, our leaders care about own benefits rather than their team's goals"*. Furthermore, most successful managers at Kazakh companies are middle-aged males. This is a result of differences between men and women, which are still visible after the collapse of the Soviet Union. Finally, for a Kazakh leader it is important to be surrounded by people who, he or she can trust because there is a lack of faith, resulting from the Soviet time (Horne, 2014). As Meijer (13 March 2018) mentions: *"The higher you come, how more important it is that you have people around you, that we call friends"*. Overall, the cooperation among leaders and subordinates is more relationship-oriented than focussed on delivering quality. In other words, it is of less importance if subordinates are capable of doing their job.

Survey results and what local respondents say

To gather more high-quality information about leadership in Kazakhstan, an online survey has been distributed to a number of Kazakh professionals who are in high positions and who have had significant experience with leadership. They share their opinions and experiences on different leadership topics, which will be summarised hereafter. People in Kazakhstan have different ideas about how a leader ought to behave. Almost all of the CCBS Survey (2018) respondents agree that a successful leader should have organisational experience. Besides that, he or she needs to have market expertise and technical competences. Next to these characteristics, employees have different expectations from of a leader. Successful leaders in Kazakhstan need to be a *"powerful decision maker"* and a *"visionary thinker"*. Additionally, having access to the right networks and a high degree of intellectuality will increase the level of success of a leader in Kazakhstan (CCBS Survey, 2018).

Nowadays, in Kazakhstan the differences between men and women remain clearly visible. A lot of Kazakh professionals indicate that senior leadership positions are not equally accessible to both genders. Mrs Geydt (CCBS Survey, 2018) elaborates regarding the characteristics of both genders: *"Women tend to compromises [sic], while men are more likely to make powerful decisions"*. Another topic in the survey discusses the input of subordinates in established procedures in a company. The survey indicates that the subordinates have to follow established procedures most of the time. If subordinates want to change the rules in order to improve their performance and achieve better results *"the rules change should be discussed with the manager first"* according to Mrs Geydt (CCBS Survey, 2018). According to the survey respondents, most leaders will be addressed by their titles rather than their first name. These titles include academic titles and leadership titles. Almost all respondents agree that *"Генеральный директор"* (General Director) is the most used leadership title in Kazakhstan followed by CEO and President. All these titles should be mentioned on your business card or in the e-mail signature.

Local leadership analysis

In-country literature review

Kazakhstan has a rich cultural history in terms of literature. In Kazakhstan poems and literature has been written and spread from generation to generation. Nevertheless, publishing literature about leadership is not a popular topic in Kazakhstan. Muktharova and Medeni (2013) write that there is a near-absence of published material on Kazakhstani school leadership in English. The local literature written about leadership is about their general leadership in the country and describes that people in Kazakhstan are overall satisfied. Most local literature elaborates on the heavily authoritarian leader, who is surrounded by his family members but takes the right decisions for the country which makes them satisfied (Gubaidulin, 2016). This is acknowledged by the research of Almaz Tolymbek. According to Tolymbek's (2007) research, the typical profile of a Kazakh political or national leader is characterised y paternalism, the position within the government hierarchy and having family ties with the ruling elite. All in all, local literature is positive about the leadership style in Kazakhstan for both leadership in companies, as well as national leadership. Kazakhs trust in the leadership style and believe that this is the best for their economy and country.

Richard A. Castleberry: a Kazakh leadership scholar

Richard A. Castleberry, the Head of Business Development for Academic Programmes at Nazarbayev University, has also been living in Kazakhstan for six years. He has been involved within different management functions in the academic world globally. Castleberry shared his experiences about Kazakh leadership characteristics in an interview (Castleberry, 12 April 2018). Firstly, he mentions that there are strong Western influences in the Kazakh academic world. Kazakh universities consist of approximately eighty percent of international students from almost fifty different nations. Therefore, the old Soviet-culture is likely to change into a more Western culture. Despite the large number of international students, the majority of involved staff remains from Kazakh origin resulting in a cultural difference between staff and students. Secondly, Castleberry highlights the role of the Kazakh president Nazarbayev in his country. The president plays an important role in the development of Kazakhstan. According to Castleberry, *"He puts Kazakhstan on the map through his initiatives, vision and activities. He sends students abroad to other countries to gain more knowledge and then return to Kazakhstan to apply this knowledge in the middle management or higher management of Kazakh companies"* (Castleberry, 12 April 2018). Finally, Castleberry notices some aspects regarding subordinates. They are more productive when the leader rules, so they need to be under pressure to obtain the desired results. Castleberry mentions that *"If you do not rule that way here, then subordinates do whatever they want to do. They need to have permission for each action they are intended to take, even if they need to go to the toilet"* (Castleberry, 12 April 2018).

Adriaan Meijer: experiencing Kazakhstani leadership

Adriaan Jan Meijer is currently involved within the Board of Directors at Air Astana as Director of Standards. Previously, he had worked as a chief pilot for KLM, was one of the founders of the airline *Dutchbird* and implemented new regulations within the aviation industry. Meijer has lived in a lot of countries, has a lot of expert experience in management positions and has been stationed in Almaty for almost a decade. Firstly, the most important message from Meijer about leadership in Kazakhstan is that having a relationship is the key factor to success. Having people around you that you trust will contribute to successful cooperation. This is influenced by the former Soviet time, during which a lot of suspicion was created (Meijer, 13 March 2018). Another topic that Meijer points out during the interview is the characteristics of leaders in Kazakhstan. They could be described as very independent and status-minded. Additionally, Meijer (13 March 2018) also underlines that *"They will not take a risk, unless they have to"*. Furthermore, the comparison among direct and indirect is difficult to understand for Kazakh leaders. It depends on the type of Kazakh, of which there are two: native Kazakhs and Russian Kazakhs. The last category will be more direct, while native Kazakhs are mainly indirect in a pleasant way. Finally, Kazakh leaders are very short-term oriented. The invitation for a meeting will not be sent a week before, but according to Meijer (13 March 2018), *"Here in Kazakhstan, it is two hours before, maybe"* and everybody is there.

In-country leadership bestseller

In 2013, one of the best-selling books about leadership in Kazakhstan, written by Daniyar Sugralinov, was published, entitled: *Kirpichi: How to Build Something from Nothing*. Although the book is seen as a leadership book, it would be better to characterise it as a motivational book. The book is about Sergei Rezvei, who builds his life from the bricks. Sergei is a man who wishes to change his life but does not know how to make it happen. Everything changes when he meets Leh, a cheerful and confident person who becomes his mentor. This mentor unfolds everything about Sergei's life and teaches him that with confidence everything can be changed. He teaches Sergei to face his difficulties and begin to work on his personal development. All the difficulties are surmountable, and at the end, they are all worth it. This book is about life-orientation, self-improvement, self-realisation, motivation, relationships and aspirations that can and should be put into practice (Rakuten kobo, n.d).

Local leadership book		
Title	**Kirpichi (Кирпичи)**	
Subtitle	Bricks	
Author	Sugralinov, Daniyar	
Publisher	Scribe Wizard lp	
Year	2013	
ISBN	1230000149643	

Kazakh leadership YouTube review

To get the most accurate results for the research about leadership in Kazakhstan, results of other professionals and researchers and their findings will be analysed as well. First of all, Maxim Maximov describes what he views as one of the key elements of leadership in Kazakhstan: encouragement (Maximov, 2015). When you want something to be achieved, it is more effective to encourage people than to punish them. Encouragement from the leader gets subordinates excited and gives them hope to do a good job.

Secondly, Alexander Pakemonov, a researcher in Kazakhstan and senior teacher at the Kazakh National University, describes more key aspects of successful Kazakh leadership in an interview for the 2016 CCBS minor programme (Minor CCBS, 2016). They are respect, cognition, authority and reputation. Of these four elements, reputation is the most important to be successful. Without a good reputation, it is impossible to have a leading position in a Kazakh company. Furthermore, Pakemonov elaborates on receiving feedback. It is appreciated to get feedback and also required to be a good leader, but as in all Asian countries, it is not respectful to give direct negative feedback. To give feedback, people describe a process in the project which went wrong. The leader or receiver should decode the message himself (Minor CCBS, 2016).

Understanding hierarchy in Kazakhstan

Kazakhstan has an extremely hierarchical society, as well as a hierarchical working environment. This hierarchic cultural behaviour is an old influence of the Communist Era of Kazakhstan. In both surroundings, people are respected because of their age and position (Commisceo-global, n.d). In the hierarchical environment it is expected that senior people, in most cases the highest position, are capable of making the right decisions due to their large amount of working experience. Therefore, most decisions will be taken by the top management of the company, while subordinates have almost no influence on the decision-making process, because of the top-down structure (Castleberry, 12 April 2018). As Meijer (13 March 2018) describes: *"A good boss listens to its group, but the boss is supposed to make the decision"*. After the decision is made, subordinates should neither contradict nor criticise the decision of the person in charge. This habit is still present in the working environments in Kazakhstan. A CEO from a Kazakh technology company emphasises that the commands of a leader are obeyed and very little room is left for the employee's self-expression (Gurbanov, 2016). For this reason, the subordinates expect the leader to fulfil an image that shows authority and to give them orders on what to do, as confirmed by Richard A. Castleberry (12 April 2018). Another specific aspect about leadership in Kazakhstan, according to Jumadildayeva (2016) is: *"that if you have a lower position it is very hard for you to get your ideas to the leader and usually person who is above you ('have more power') is the one to decide the most"*.

Lastly, for subordinates in Kazakhstan it is not common to address their managers by their first names. Moreover, when employees need to talk or inform their managers, they should address their leader according to their title or positions to approach them. Professionals who took part in the CCBS Survey (2018) suggest that this is becoming more flexible nowadays, because of increasing globalisation, particularly in society (CCBS Survey, 2018). All in all, hierarchy is still a key aspect in a Kazakh working environment and society.

How Kazakhstani achieve leadership empathy

According to Low (2012), there are five key elements in achieving leadership empathy: communicating with employees, collaborating with employees, coaching employees, caring about employees and controlling them. As a Kazakh leader, this all comes together in being fatherly. It contains caring and showing concern for your employees, but also about the working environment of the employees. The CCBS Survey (2018) indicates that, for a Kazakh leader, it is important to have *"a strong charismatic personality"*. Then employees will feel motivated and appreciated. In order to achieve empathy as a leader in Kazakhstan, face-to-face relationships with subordinates are very important. The majority of the professionals (CCBS Survey, 2018) indicate that a manager should spend time on the well-being of team members. Moreover, a leader could empathise with his or her subordinates when the leader sees things from their perspective. Therefore, a meeting always starts by building a relationship in a formal way. Lewis (2006) highlights another way of achieving empathy, such as showing your knowledge and skills to subordinates, wearing formal clothing, which contributes to professionalism, and being involved in the subordinates' activities. This gives a leader the possibility to both motivate and give feedback. Giving feedback is another key element in achieving leadership empathy. It is not common for an employee to give feedback to his or her manager, but the other way around. This as a result from the hierarchical structure within an organisation, in which subordinates should have respect for their leaders. Feedback will be given by a leader, frequently during a meeting in an indirect way, to strengthen the relationship with subordinates. When subordinates want to give feedback to their leader, it will mostly happen outside the meeting and also in an indirect way (Meijer, 13 March 2018).

Kenya

Giles Agbenyoh, Frederike van den Brande & Lars Smithuis

Believed to be the 'Cradle of Mankind' the country where life emerged as we know it, Kenya, also known as *Kīrīnyaga* (*Kikuyu* dialect) meaning 'one having stripes', is located in East Africa (Barsby, 2017). It covers an area slightly larger than France and is home to 47 million inhabitants, of which the majority resides in the rural areas, the capital Nairobi, and coastal city Mombasa. Kenya is situated on the equator and shares its borders with five countries: Uganda, Sudan, Somalia, Ethiopia and Tanzania. Kenya is an ethnically diverse country and includes indigenous tribal cultures, such as the Masaai and Samburu tribes, who live in close harmony with nature and are characterised by their traditional lifestyle and attitude. Kenya's official national languages are English and Swahili. However, each ethnic group has its own dialect, with Bantu and Kikuyu being the most common ones, as the vast majority practices them. Kenya is a popular tourist destination due to its geographical diversity. With some of the continent's most pristine landscapes, the country ranges from mountains to forests, coastlines with beaches and wide-open savannahs with a wide range of different animal species.

Kenya is often perceived as the regional hub of East Africa, due to the strategic location of Mombasa's seaport, which is one of the most utilized along the African coastline. The national currency is the Kenyan Shilling, and Kenyan export is comprised of agricultural related products, such as tea, fruits, flora, coffee and vegetables (KPMG, 2017). Kenya is set to be among the most advanced economies in Africa as there has been continuous expanding wealth across different sectors including telecommunications, agriculture and tourism that act as main drivers of the Kenyan economy.

How the Kenyans characterise leaders

In Kenya, there is much diversity in ethnic, religious and gender dimensions. Therefore, Kenyan leader characteristics are sub-divided and are dependent on different variables, such as region, rank and sector (Wambui, Wangombe & Jackson, 2013). For instance, the age at which Kenyans can assume a leadership role is somewhat dependent on the sector. Corporate and governmental leaders are mainly middle-aged. However, within the informal sector and Small and Medium Enterprises (SME's), locally referred to as the *Jua Kali* (Kiswahili) meaning 'hot sun', the majority of leaders are young to middle-aged. In the political environment, leaders are often middle-aged to elderly (Kahando, Maina & Mweru, 2017). Kobia (4 April 2018) explains that political leaders are mostly elderly because of their perceived wisdom and the high campaign costs. *"Increasing your chances of being elected to a political leadership position requires financial muscle"*. First, you need to accumulate the appropriate amount of funds, which is more likely to be realised during that age category.

While the leadership attributes also differ across sectors there are some that they have in common. Research conducted by Mwangi, Sejjaaka, Canny and Maina (2016) examines the success of leaders in the SMEs and corporate sectors. The results suggest that effective leaders have a clear vision, team-building capabilities, the ability to motivate staff and extensive knowledge of the field they operate in. This implies that Kenyans believe that leaders earned their position because they are more competent than those they lead. One of the CCBS Survey (2018) respondents specifically indicates that a track-record of leadership-related activities is among the most important qualities of a leader. Although the stereotypical Kenyan leader is associated with the male gender and masculinity, Kenya is making progress compared to surrounding countries in having more women in top leadership positions (Amondi, 2010). This is especially true after the entrance of the latest constitution, which calls for increased gender equity, giving women equal rights to men. This constitution also urges leaders to take more responsibility regarding diversity inclusion for a united Kenya (Counsil Kenya, 2010). The presented leadership model in the book: *Challenging the Rulers* by Okombo, Kwaka, Muluka and Nyabuto (2011) describes that to be a politically effective leader in Kenya, one should create a culture of accountability, ensure that decisions are made in democracy and enable followers to realise their full potential in society. Taking all elements into consideration, it can be said that Kenyan leaders are mainly characterised by their demographical features, expertise and endeavours to be ethically correct.

Local leadership analysis

In-country literature review

In Kenya, there is a wide perception of what can be defined as good leadership. Firstly, Kenya's most employed leadership style is transactional in nature, which indicates that leaders are often task-oriented and authoritarian (Mberia &

Midigo, 2016). Usually, subordinates prefer to engage with peers from the same ethnic group and will try to favour their own interests (Lituchy, Galperin & Punnett, 2017). Therefore, leaders often opt to maintain an objective attitude with a focus on clear-set targets that need to be achieved; they expect orders to be obeyed without question to avoid conflicts and keep harmony. However, research conducted by Kihara (2016) indicates that the opposing trans-formational leadership style, which provides more freedom and empowers subordinates to be engaged during decision-making, actually has a significant positive impact on performance within Kenyan firms. This outcome is also supported by research from Minja (2010) regarding job satisfaction since all survey respondents indicated that empowerment, motivation, integrity, and concern for the well-being of employees are amongst the important values and traits that a leader should possess for effective leadership in Kenya. Kobia (4 April 2018) confirms the literature findings with *"leaders in Kenya should be approachable, and able to listen to the ones they are leading. Every opinion counts"*.

Ethical leadership involves having personal values, endeavouring for mutuality, making the right decision regardless of the situation and creating a framework that enables your followers to benefit from adequate decision-making. It all relates to ethical leadership, which remains a challenge in African countries, and Kenya is no exception (Minja, 2017). Once elected to a leadership position in Kenya, especially in the political arena, a person is exposed to a lot of power. Leadership positions in Kenya are accompanied by wealth, prestige and unquestioned authority privileges. As a result, there is a lot of self-enrichment, and Kenyan leaders often refuse to relinquish power (Kagema, 2018). In addition, Kobia (4 April 2018) states that *"[o]nce you are chosen [for] a leader position in Kenya, it is associated with power. Unfortunately, there is a lack of responsibility."* During a service of pastor and leadership counsellor, Simon Mbevi, he defined ethical leadership in Kenya by preaching for moral integrity. He defined an ethical leader as someone who loves and promotes peace and who bridges the divides of the nation (Ogutu, 2014).

Joel Mwenda Kobia: a Kenyan cross-cultural trainer

Mr Joel Mwenda Kobia is an expert in the field of leadership training and consultancy. Furthermore, he is a life coach, motivational speaker, and financial consultant. He holds a Master's in Business Administration (Strategic Leadership) and served in various national and international leadership positions. Also, he is the author of the book *Between Me and My Exploits* (2017) wherein he guides his readers to a positive mindset in seeking opportunities. Based on his experience, Kobia is the ideal person to interview for a comprehensive perspective on leadership in Kenya. According to Kobia (4 April 2018), the most utilised leadership style in Kenya is dictatorial and based on formal rules and regulations in order to guide subordinates to accomplish their targets. In general, leadership styles are transactional and more task-oriented in nature. However, recently there has been a lot more employee empowerment, which has translated into subordinates being much more involved in the decision-making process. Kobia encourages this development as incorporating different perspectives enriches a leader's mindset. Within the political arena of Kenya, gender and ethnic diversity play a significant role since the country is guided by tribal subdivisions and groupings, and leadership consists of coalitions between different major tribes. Kobia (4 April 2018) mentions that tribalism currently causes tension in the country, especially in the political sector. Nonetheless, he stresses that political leaders under the current regime try to aim for mutual agreements. Kobia pleads for enhanced nationhood by stating *"We never have to forget that Kenya is greater than all of us"* (4 April 2018).

Regarding developments in the field of leadership consultancy, Kobia (4 April 2018) notes that firms are allocating higher budgets towards leadership training and workshops. Also, leadership training is not merely focused on the top positions anymore and has increasingly involved all organisational ranks. This requires them to cooperate during these sessions, naturally enhancing the team bonding. His words of wisdom for emerging Kenyan leaders is to employ a hybrid of the egalitarian (transformational) leadership style with the task-oriented (transactional) style, while simultaneously being a visionary and a good motivator (Kobia, 4 April 2018). Most fundamentally, in order to achieve good and effective leadership, Kenyans should take responsibility for the power that is associated with leadership. Instead of self-enrichment and preserving power, they should focus on servant-leadership and ensure the well-being and interests of the ones that they lead. In conclusion, Kobia (4 April 2018) adds: *"It is difficult to become an effective leader in Kenya, if you are not able to lead yourself."*

In-country leadership bestseller

Olonana Ole Mbatian is considered to be one of the most remarkable and influential leaders in Masaai and Kenyan history. Native author Peter Ndege writes the book named after this leader, published in 2003. It covers his biography by engaging the reader through different inspirational events of his life. Where traditional leadership literature focuses on theoretical concepts, Peter Ndege aims to educate his readers by providing insights on how Olonana became a respected leader during a period of nation building, colonial occupation and envy for wealth and power. During Olonana's spell as tribal leader of the *Masaai* during the nineteenth century, he strived for social cohesion based on ethical leadership. The key message conveyed is that being a Kenyan leader requires the ability to spread a feeling of mutuality among everyone you guide. *"In our culture, there is no such expression as being a stranger. You are welcome."* Essentially, the book has become an eye-opener for students and emerging Kenyan leaders as it advocates for a more united Kenya that in modern days is marked by tribalism rather than nationhood.

Local leadership book	
Title	Olonana Ole Mbatian
Author	-
Author	Peter Ndege
Publisher	East African Educational Publishers, Kenya
Year	2003
ISBN	9789966250940

Kenyan leadership YouTube review

The focus point of the video interview, *building good leadership in Kenya and learning how to pay it forward*, is on the next generation of emerging Kenyan leaders. It focuses on the Kenyan youth between the ages of 22 and 25. Kenyan inhabitants believe that it is important for the youth not only to love their country but also to love themselves and be able to exploit opportunities.

Leadership is much more than just a position or status; a leader should be able to identify how they can inspire and take into consideration the aspirations of the ones they lead. Currently, Kenyan youth has the perception that leadership is associated with increased financial gains, while the true value of leadership is measured by the satisfaction gained from helping others to reach their full potential. At the moment, there is a lack of dialogue between high ranked leaders and the youth. The government should stimulate discussion on leadership. By, for example, providing a platform where they are able to speak their minds and exchange ideas about leadership-related topics (NTV Kenya, 2017).

Understanding hierarchy in Kenya

Kenyan society has a high level of power distance. People understand and accept their place in the system, and they expect to be told what the higher ranked want from them. The hierarchal structure within Kenya is often based on a vertical framework, with a top-down decision-making process (Oloko & Ogutu, 2012). However, firms are emerging where superiors prefer their subordinates to call them by their first name, whereas most bosses are still more traditional. *"Some companies are still old-fashioned in this aspect especially where quasi-government institutions are involved"*, explains a respondent of the CCBS Survey (2018). This change is also reflected in a comment by Jonathan Somen, founder and CEO of multiple Kenyan companies. *"Kenya is more traditional still with many older businesses but in my business, I insist on first names"* (CCBS Survey, 2018). Although, in general orders from superiors need to be adhered to, employees may offer their own ideas and vision on a case. The CCBS Survey (2018) respondent, Jonathan Somen, agrees: *"If employees have better solutions or can improve the rules to make them better, then we expect them to come forward and present their ideas on improvement."* According to leadership consultant, Joel M. Kobia, there is an upcoming trend that input from subordinates is more and more accepted and even expected from modern leaders, which in his eyes complies with the trend that average age in Kenya for leaders is decreasing (Kobia, 4 April 2018).

Additionally, gender is a significant aspect to the hierarchical structure as women are generally ranked lower in the system than men (Kamau, 2010). Although, female leaders are increasingly being accepted in society. An example of that is the Nairobi Leadership Academy, which is a private boarding and day school that prepares young women to excel both academically and professionally (NLA, 2018). Professionals who responded to the CCBS Survey (2018) confirm that equality is coming but is not there yet. Leadership consultant, Eric Juma Swaleh, states in the survey that *"women are known to have greater concern for people"* (CCBS Survey, 2018). On the other hand, entrepreneur Westeykoech thinks that *"men's leadership is more productive than that of women"* (CCBS Survey, 2018). Visions of gender equality are varied, as some other survey respondents state that they do not see any differences in leadership styles in men and women (CCBS Survey, 2018).

How Kenyans achieve leadership empathy

Achieving empathy when assigned to a leadership position in Kenya is realised by taking into account different cultural aspects. Primarily, leaders should be aware of the high collectivism, implying that Kenyan leaders should have a high sense of responsibility for the well-being and cohesion of subordinates (Kessler & Wong-MingJi, 2009). For example, in order for a change to be implemented, the idea needs to be perceived as good for the collective, so nobody feels offended or harmed during the process (Kihara, Ngugi & Ogollah, 2016).

Therefore, from a leadership perspective, empathy is realised by being responsive to the needs, concerns and interests of the ones you lead. This requires leaders to be engaged and to maintain personal relationships with their employees. However, relationships in the corporate and political sectors remain on a more professional level (Kobia, 4 April 2018). Maintaining close relationships with subordinates also relates to the ethical concept named *Ubuntu*, that can be expressed as "humanness, or being human". It entails that leaders should ensure no one falls too far behind from the group and that a leader should act as a unifying factor, bringing subordinates together regardless of their background or status (Lutz, 2009). Furthermore, Kenyans are open and hospitable people; therefore, appropriate communication and interaction are vital elements when seeking affinity. A leader should attempt to avoid blunt statements when providing feedback. Even if considered constructive, leaders should make an effort to communicate indirectly as public exposure will lead to a decline in respect (Mwangi, Sejjaaka, Canny & Maina, 2016).

A CCBS Survey (2018) respondent indicates that the main difference between Kenyan and Western leadership practices lies in the communication style: *"Cultural nuances are important to understand. [For example] silence does not mean consent like is practiced in European countries where people are open and direct."* Instead, leaders gain empathy by addressing their issues in a more discreet manner.

Moreover, when being assigned to a leadership position in Kenya, one must understand that subordinates should be approached as a community, not as individuals. This is magnified by the so-called *Harambee* fund, which is meant to support a good cause and to stimulate cohesion of communities. Translated it means "let's all work together" and is widely adopted within Kenya (Koshal, 2005). In conclusion, leadership empathy is achieved by focusing on the success of one employee in regard to the success of the collective.

Korea, Republic of

Juno Beckers, Robin Bol & Frank Eriks

South Korea, officially the Republic of Korea or as spelt in the native Hangul script 대한민국, is a flourishing country located in the far east of Asia. The Republic of Korea is one of the denser populated countries on the planet with more than 50 million inhabitants (Euromonitor, 2018). The main language of the country is Korean, which is classified as one of the Altaic languages (Lew, Yu, Lee, Im & Hanh, 2018). The Republic of Korea is also a relatively young country with the first republic only being established in August 1948. After the Korean War (during the 1950s), its economy was weak and devastated. Interestingly enough though, Korea's economy has been strengthening since the sixties, with rapidly growing industries, targeting textile and light manufacturing. This was achieved by focusing on industrial industries, rather than more traditional agricultural industries. Due to this, Korea saw a major increase in the middle-class population (Lew et al., 2018). Nowadays, Korea is synchronized by the rhythm of K-pop and a glass of Soju. It is known for producing high-technology products, with global active brands, such as Samsung Electronics, LG and Hyundai Motors. With a focus on export, Korea has achieved a high Gross Domestic Product (GDP) comparable to countries like Russia, Canada and Brazil (Euromonitor, 2018). Despite the globalisation of Korea, the local population still cherishes and highly respects its traditions. Every person, on every social level, has his or her title, which reflects the strong hierarchy and status-consciousness; this does not only apply to relatives and friends but also extends to the business sphere (Kim, B'lyou & Wang, 2017).

How the Koreans characterise leaders

Korean leaders are characterised by implementing a task-driven style in their way of leading a company or team. The manager is responsible for steering and instructing a team, but together they will work towards the best possible results (Won-Shul & Steers, 2001). A Korean leader should, according to the CCBS Survey (2018), be a visionary, a listener and a professional decision maker. The person should have a charismatic personality, a working network, political connections and a high intellect. Koreans will look up to a leader who has organisational and market experience. Besides all these qualities one of the most important requirements is one's age. This is due to the fact that according to Korean standards, a leader should be older than his or her subordinates (Greaves, 30 March 2018). Where in Western countries younger leaders are a regular scene, in Korea it is almost non-existent. Mr Greaves (30 March 2018) explains how this is perceived in South Korea: *"You don't get younger people in charge, for instance, it never happens, [...] the person in charge cannot understand [how to be in charge], because they haven't reached that level of [maturity] where they can be put in charge."*. Another key characteristic that a leader should possess is being paternalistic; this means that the leader acts as a parent towards his or her team as if they are part of the leader's family. *"Family atmosphere is crucial to the Korean business environment, so they are constantly considering their business partners"* (Videoinfographs, 2013). This leadership style is established from the Chinese Confucianism, which emphasises respect for elders, loyalty to your supervisor and the importance of family (especially that the youth should support the elderly in the family) (Carar & Kim, 2015).

If we venture further into the higher hierarchy of a company, the leader of a company would be recognisable by his or her more formal clothing style. Santos (2015) explains that the typical business attire for Korean leaders is a white shirt and conservative dark suit. A leader in Korea is expected to show his or her status; this expresses their authority. Status is reflected in the earlier noted clothing style, but also by a suitable workspace and a luxury car (CCBS Survey, 2018). Many Koreans are inwardly jealous of this image and will do everything to please their boss, with the goal of ultimately reaching the same status as him or her. A manager is keen on keeping his or her image as desirable as possible. When something weakens their image, they are unlikely to reach that desirable level again; this also harms his or her leadership capabilities (Estes, 2012).

Survey results and what local respondents say

The CCBS Survey that has been conducted over the past two years has generated an interesting perspective from locals into some of the leadership aspects. The CCBS Survey (2018), which was filled in by more than fifty people, points out three main topics. The first is regarding the working ethics, the second is about power distance and the developments and the third and final point is the difference between men and women, in the context of business leadership.

In terms of work ethics, employees in Korea are used to working hard and closely obeying the instructions of their supervisors. For example, you should not openly criticise your superior; this always has to be done indirectly according to almost 60 percent of the respondents. From the leader's side, this is a different story, and over 60 percent agree that a manager should be able to openly address his or her employees if this is necessary to reach a goal. A competitive working environment is also preferred by most of the respondents, resulting in a better final result. More than 50 percent agree that when the goal is reached, it is final and cannot be changed afterwards. With the final point on work ethics, regarding the importance of a deadline, nearly ninety percent agree that missing a deadline is seen as a failure (CCBS Survey, 2018).

One of the most different cultural aspects is the equality, or better said inequality, between men and women in South Korea. On the statement in the survey concerning if men and women have equal access to senior positions, more than half of the respondents in the survey voted 'disagree' and just a little over one fifth 'fully agreed'. A Korean coordinator added the following: "*Women tend not to promote at their work because when they become a mother, they have to raise the child and therefore their career will discontinue*" (CCBS Survey, 2018). This is confirmed by a news article of *The Dong-A Ilbo* (2012) where it is argued that the wage gap in Korea is to blame on the high number of women who quit their jobs in order to raise their children. Another respondent adds that "*[the hierarchical structure] is influenced by old-school men and women, their attitudes are from patriarchy*" (CCBS Survey, 2018).

The masculinity that males bring in leadership is currently really sought after. Besides, a local researcher points out that social and infrastructural factors prohibit women to fulfil a higher position. This despite both genders having equal opportunities (CCBS Survey, 2018). Despite the fact that women face a clear disadvantage in the Korean business environment, a current trend is developing in which women leaders in business are on the increase. The CFO of a Korean Bio-Pharmaceutical company states that this is partly because women tend to work on a closer relationship basis with their employees, rather than the old-fashioned hierarchy (CCBS Survey, 2018). This closer contact between management and employees is highly valued, and this feminine form of leadership is likely to be seen more in the near future (Greaves, 30 March 2018).

Local leadership analysis

In-country literature review

An interesting article about current day leadership in Korea can be found in the Korean newspaper: *Dongyang Daily News.* In this article, a professor of the Shinsung University (신성 대학교), writes about leadership viewed from a Chinese perspective. The book, titled *성공하는 리더를 위한 중국고전 12편* (*12 Chinese Classics for Successful Leaders*) written by Japan's Hiroshi Moriya (2002) is used as a basis for his research. In this article, the importance of harmony and mutual trust between co-worker and leader is highlighted. The respect that Koreans have for elders and the brotherly love they show for one another is used as an example of this harmony on the work floor (기원, 2013). This corresponds with the family atmosphere which is crucial in Korean business environment and underlines the importance of this.

Contrary to the above newspaper article, an article written for the Korean messaging platform, Jandi, is based on the work of a Western psychologist and researcher, Harry Levirson. This article covers the subject of how leaders should lead co-workers. It speaks of a psychological contract between leader and co-worker. In this metaphorical, psychological contract, leaders should recognise co-workers as partners, both working in harmony to achieve the same goals, recognising and respecting that each individual quality is key to achieving the best results possible (Jandi, 2016). Considering both articles are based on different perspectives, the base view of Koreans on leaders is the same. The leaders or managers in a company have a duty to keep the harmony between co-workers on the work floor.

Huang Fei: a Korean leadership scholar

Professor Huang Fei is a South Korean Assistant Business School Professor. In an interview, Huang Fei goes more in-depth about the influence on Korean business culture from both the Confucius Chinese culture and the Western culture. She explains that the Korean business culture traditionally has been influenced by the Confucius Chinese culture. After 1948 though, Western influences started having a bigger impact on the Korean business culture.

The influences from both cultures give the Koreans an advantage in global business. Huang Fei (6 November 2017) underpins this argument with the following statement "*[This] type is more like mixed up model which forms the dynamic and fast-changing, speed-oriented business culture.*"

Besides this it also gives the Korean business environment a dynamic twist where employees tend to lean more to the traditional culture or to the western culture; *"If that person appears to be more liberal, he is prone to be more innovative. If he tends to be obedient, then he tends to be more traditional"* (Fei, 6 November 2017).

Alain Greaves: a Korean cross-cultural trainer

Alain Greaves is an international business communication consultant in Korea, which means that he helps Korean companies with their communication skills and to be more efficient in their use of English in presentations and intercultural- and cross-cultural-negotiation skills. He explains that the Koreans are reasonable in their English but do not use it effectively. This is where Alain's services come in. In Korea, the rule is the older you are, the more suitable you are to become a leader in a company. Or as Greaves (30 March 2018) implies *"if you are a leader, you are a leader because you are older than the others and therefore you can control them, and they will follow what you say. It's very very different from the leadership that we expect in Western countries."*

The hierarchical culture originates from the military. Here people get instructions, and they need to follow these instructions. After the military service, Korean employees and employers tend to use this hierarchical structure in the business environment. As Greaves (30 March 2018) explains: *"They have given instructions, and they follow the instruction*s." Because of this, employees are generally not encouraged to come-up with their own ideas.

In-country leadership bestseller

According to Korean respondents (CCBS Survey, 2018) on the survey, one of the best-selling books about leadership was written by 고현숙 (Helen Hyonsook Ko) in 2017 and is called *결정적 순간의 리더십* (Decisive moments of leadership). 고현숙 has over 15 years' experience in coaching leaders in large cooperations like Samsung and LG. In the book, she explains the strategies and the secrets about *Decisive moments of leadership*. The book is full of guidelines and mindsets about the competence of a successful leader in a Korean enterprise and answers various questions like what the role of a leader is in an organisation and how to lead a company to success and growth by utilising all members' potential (Daum, n.d.).

Local leadership book	
Title	결정적 순간의 리더십
Subtitle	-
Author	고현숙
Publisher	Sam & Parkers
Year	2017
ISBN	9788965704256

Korean leadership YouTube review

According to Don Southerton (CEO and President of Bridging Cultures Worldwide and author of *Korea Facing: Secrets for Success in Korean Global Business*), the old management system has its origin from the old government system in combination with the military regime. In the seventies, eighties and nineties the government was in charge of most companies. They decided what the companies were going to produce, in what quantities and where they were going to produce it. Southerton (2013) describes this as *"an authoritarian bureaucratic management system"*.

But, Southernton (2013) also explains that this is changing *"It has been a paradigm shift in Korea from that old hardest model to what we call a softer model, from a top-down where there's no communication going back up to a collaborative mode"*. The younger generation realised that they needed to be more international and acted on that by being more collaborative. Nowadays, they listen a lot to other business cultures and get more opinions from other people to act better on a globalising market. Thus, they have adopted a more open culture.

Understanding hierarchy in Korea

One major point that defines the hierarchical structure is the respect for elders (Facts, 1991). This mostly results in older people having a higher position, regardless of whether they have the same skill-set as younger people. According to Greaves (30 March 2018), even one day makes a difference in the hierarchy: *"If you are born one day later than somebody else, then you are that person's junior and you have to follow them."* Given the fact that seniority is so heavily respected, it is no surprise that the hierarchical structure remains firm. The reason for this is mostly because all male Koreans have endured this during their mandatory military service (CCBS Survey, 2018). Since this military-hierarchical structure is a big influence on corporate-hierarchy, power distance between the top and low-ranking personnel is very high (Greaves, 30 March 2018). According to one of our respondents, this is heavily influenced by the mandatory military service. The respondent describes this state of affairs as follows: *"The old (senior) are above the young (junior), this style originates from the military services most men have endured."* (CCBS Survey, 2018). People are given instructions, and they have to follow them. Employees have little to no input. The employees are often afraid to speak up to their management, and communication usually flows one way. As Yoon (2012) notes, employees can speak as much as they want, but they are unlikely to receive a response. More typically, the workforce takes orders from their management with no further questions.

Another historical aspect of Korean hierarchy is the importance placed on family name and wealth. Korea is a typical top-down society, which means that when power is usually given it is not easily amended (Southerton, 2013). This is probably most evident for the Chaebols family, which is a Korean business group controlled by one Korean family. This family has been influential ever since the Korean industrial revolution of the sixties. With strong connections to the government, this family plays a key role in the Korean economy, but the Chaebols were not always known for being fair. Back in the eighties, they were even accused of abusing their power (Jun, Sheldon & Ree, 2010). Even though more than ninety percent of the CCBS Survey (2018) state that family background and family connections are not key-aspects of a leader in Korean working culture, it cannot be ignored that the family name and wealth are important parts of the hierarchy in Korean business history.

How Koreans achieve leadership empathy

Given that Korea is being influenced more and more by other cultures, their traditions and social status are still a huge part of the culture (Greaves, 30 March 2018). Take for example the term *Kibun* (기분). This plays an important role in leadership empathy. *Kibun* is a mood or a feeling of balance and good behaviour. In the Business world, Korean people always try to be polite, friendly and do things with only the best of intentions. Leaders do not want others to lose face by criticising them in public. A manager's *Kibun* is damaged if his or her subordinates do not show proper respect (Santos, 2015). Etiquette in this is immensely important. When asked if it is important to address leaders by their titles, the vast majority of our respondents said this should always or often be done (CCBS Survey, 2018). According to Mr Chung, the proper way to address a leader is by his surname and title(s) (CCBS Survey, 2018).

In return for showing this respect, subordinates expect that a leader takes care of them. The results of the CCBS survey show that almost 80 percent of the respondents agree with the fact that the manager should actively spend time on the personal well-being of team members (CCBS Survey, 2018). Senior Learning and Organisation Development manager of CJ America (a large Korean conglomerate), Seog Joo Wong (18 April 2018), states in an interview that *"If you are good leadership with good expertise, charisma, and caring mind for your employees, they will like and follow you as their uncle or father."* This again reflects on the earlier discussed paternalistic role.

On the other hand, a leader expects from their subordinates that they are dedicated to their work and that they are open to new ideas. Many Koreans are creative and love to show initiative if needed (Inanlou & Ji-Young, 2017). Another way to achieve empathy is by sharing a mutual sense of humour. Although a sense of humour can help with achieving empathy, it is important to maintain a positive, substantial and business-like attitude to remain respected in a Korean working environment (Kim, Lee, Wong & Shan, 2016).

Nigeria

Elske Wismeier, Eve Lochhead & Tirsa Haaswijk

Nigeria is a federal republic which is known for its scenic cities, large oil reserves, and natural beauty. With about 200 million inhabitants, it is Africa's most populous country. The official language of Nigeria is English, although a surprising 520 languages are spoken. The most common ones include Hausa, Igbo and Yoruba. This African gem is home to many different religions, although Islam and Christianity are the dominant ones. Nigeria is currently undergoing economic and political changes, which often practically influence doing business. The country experiences a lot of corruption, and over 70% of the population lives under the poverty line. In spite of all this the country is progressing towards a better future, by improving the standard of living and encouraging development. Nigeria is home to some of the most light-hearted people in the world, which makes it an unparagoned travel destination. The national culture prioritises taking care of its citizens. Furthermore, culture is a highly-valued aspect, and it needs to be respected in social and professional contexts. This bears implications for the ideal Nigerian leader; such a leader should be strong, have a clear vision and be warm-hearted towards his or her employees.

How Nigerians characterise leaders

In Nigeria, a good leader is expected to possess excellent communication skills and the ability to express his or her vision clearly (Aipoh, 16 March 2018). In addition, successful leaders convey genuine integrity and sincerity. Nigerian people value respect highly in business. Therefore, it is imperative to avoid embarrassing or disrespecting colleagues, especially in front of others (Moran, Harris & Moran, 2011). In showing disrespect, a person may risk damaging the business relationship permanently as Nigerians take this behaviour seriously. Furthermore, leaders who have succeeded in Nigeria have gained their respect by demonstrating the will to change in order to meet organisational goals. Being a leader is not about being viewed as a superior human; instead, it is about understanding and listening to the needs of the people and acting accordingly (CCBS Survey, 2018). According to Aipoh (16 March 2018): *"a Nigerian leader must be willing to improve the lives of the people."* Isado (21 March 2018) also states that: *"a Nigerian leader requires a positive attitude due to Nigeria's political and economic situation."* When actions are being taken, a leader is expected to show optimism about the business environment (Isado, 21 March 2018). Being a good listener is one of the best characteristics a Nigerian leader can have (CCBS Survey, 2018). According to Ejimabo (2013), it is important for leaders to first identify and understand their own values. Thereafter, they have to share these values with their followers through their behaviour, taking special care to consistently live out their values. Additionally, a good leader with a vision should be in the position to inspire and mobilise his or her employees (Ehusani, n.d). Successful leaders are polite and friendly to their colleagues; however, they must remain firm and assertive. Finally, business negotiations could be lengthy, and in order to secure a deal, Nigerian leaders must be able to compromise and adjust their expectations accordingly.

Survey results and what local respondents say

Many CCBS Survey (2018) respondents see a unique leadership style in Nigeria. Creative director, Motilayo Williams says: *"Leaders are less proud. It's good to be a leader, but it doesn't necessarily make you better than the rest"* (CCBS Survey, 2018). More than half of the respondents confirm that managers should actively spend time on the well-being of their employees (CCBS Survey, 2018). This finding is consistent with Aipoh's contention that Nigerian societies are highly collective, meaning that a leader must have the interests and well-being of people at heart. Besides this, the greater number of respondents endorse that employees must not bend the rules to achieve the results they seek. Sogelola Oluwakayode, a human resource manager, points out that: *"you can make some changes using your discretion but you must inform your boss prior [to the] time"* (CCBS Survey, 2018). Lastly, success is often related to age in Nigeria. As a Nigerian deputy manager puts it: *"Leadership in Nigeria could be very much linked with age and experience which also could be the person's wealth of knowledge, hardly will you see a young man as an overall leader (CEO) except if it is a family company/business, which is not common"* (CCBS Survey, 2018).

Local leadership analysis

In-country literature review

In his book on Nigerian leadership, Ejimabo (2013) explains that company-management is not the main purpose of Nigerian leaders. They simultaneously care about the employee's well-being and assist them in developing their own potential. Furthermore, culture is the main aspect that needs to be respected by the person in charge. There must be an understanding of the traditions, customs and languages, governing all Nigerians, regardless of their differences. To be a respectable leader, one needs to have perseverance and the capability to overcome the challenges of Nigeria (Irouma, 2018). Obi (2018) claims that: *"leadership starts and ends with service, Nigerians need to realize this"*.

R.M. Ojokuku: a Nigerian leadership scholar

In a recent Nigerian leadership study, Dr Ojokuku from the Ladoke Akintola University of Technology (LAUTECH), in Ogbomoso, Nigeria, co-authored an article in which the impact of leadership style dimensions on organisational performance in the Ibadan financial sector is examined. The findings show a positive correlation between leadership style dimensions and organisational performance, where transformational and democratic leadership styles were employed by the management (Ojokuku, Odetayo & Sajuyigbe, 2012). Ojokuku's academic research reveals that by belonging to a healthy community and allowing employees to carry higher responsibilities, organisational efficiency in Nigeria can be enhanced. In this way, followers are also aided in developing their own visions for personal development (Ojokuku et al., 2012). An autocratic leadership style, on the other hand, has a less significant effect on performance. These practices ensure a proper level of respect; however, it neglects the insight that other figures within the organisation could provide. Nigerians' ability to be collectively creative should not be underestimated. As Eddy Isado, a Nigerian business consultant shares in an interview with CCBS: *"Nigerians can be very creative in working out business ideas and transforming them into business opportunities"* (Isado, 24 March 2018).

Shirley Aipoh: a Nigerian cross-cultural trainer

Shirley Aipoh is a Nigerian cross-cultural trainer and founder of the company Global Cultures Consult. Miss Aipoh was born and raised in Nigeria, and her expertise involves cross-cultural consultancy work for African and Western

European cultures. In an interview, she notes that business opportunities in Nigeria are almost unlimited, as its vast market is rapidly expanding. Aipoh (16 March 2018) states: *"Nigerian people are able to make business projects to reach full potential due to their commitment, excitement and passion."* She also explains that working with Nigerians can be rewarding due to the commitment and passion they bring to a project. Organisations in Nigeria can vary in terms of hierarchy. Therefore, in some organisations, it is possible to have a personal relationship between a leader and an employee, without intimidation. On the other hand, a strong hierarchy can be noticed within more traditional Nigerian companies. Furthermore, Aipoh (16 March 2018) explains that a business cannot function successfully without mutual respect. If there is a lack thereof, business relationships could become difficult to handle and tension can increase. Leadership in Nigeria is about being part of a collective society and taking steps to improve the lives of the people, as opposed to making individual decisions with selfish reasoning behind them.

In-country leadership bestseller
One of the best-selling books about Nigerian leadership was written by Onyema Nkwocha in 2012: *Effective Leadership in Nigeria: Practical Ways to Build Effective, Inspiring, Transformational and Visionary Leadership and Governance in Nigeria.* This book shows practical ways to implement and inspire effective leadership.

Local leadership book	
Title	**Effective Leadership in Nigeria**
Author	Practical Ways to Build Effective, Inspiring, Transformational and Visionary Leadership and Governance in Nigeria
Author	Onyema Nkwocha
Publisher	AuthorHouse
Year	2012
ISBN	1468506781

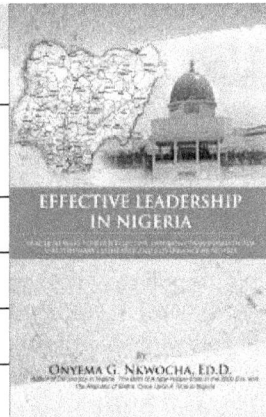

Nigerian leadership YouTube review

Many Nigerian public figures, authors and business people have voiced strong opinions over the years, on what effective leadership consists of. A common prerequisite is determination. As national coordinator for Youth Arise in Nigeria, L. Barr (2017), puts it: *"a Nigerian leader needs to possess a vision in order to be a good leader."* Furthermore, leadership consultant, Sam Adeyemi, observes that *"the essence of leadership is offering a service"* (Adeyemi, 2015). This refers again to the notion that African culture is more collectivistic rather than individualistic. Within that cultural context, leadership could mean a lot more to people – if successfully implemented, effective management could translate into social benefits for employees.

Adeyemi (2015) brings forward some interesting thoughts on Nigerian leadership. One of them suggests that maintaining a quality level of leadership requires a balance between character (personality traits) and professional competencies. The most important traits include integrity, valuing honesty and having genuine love for the people. Naturally, this establishes understanding and proper communication on organisational levels. The professional competencies, on the other hand, are needed to provide a leader with actual knowledge of the tasks at hand. Adeyemi mentions religion as another important factor in business circles in Nigeria. Many leaders use religious concepts within management and behave in accordance with Islam or Christianity (Adeyemi, 2015).

Interestingly, Adegbenro (2018) notes that Nigerians are very dissatisfied with the manner in which leadership is executed these days. He states that leadership seems to be in need of a different approach for the future (Adegbenro, 2018).

Understanding hierarchy in Nigeria

Respecting hierarchy is an inseparable part of doing business in Nigeria. To ensure the proper levels of hierarchy are maintained, leaders should be respected by having their position and status within the business acknowledged (Isado, 21 March 2018). Hence, Nigerian leaders cannot be addressed by their first name (CCBS Survey, 2018). Seniority is also essential to doing business in Nigeria, which is also related to the Nigerian value for respect (CCBS Survey, 2018). Most managers are from an older generation because citizens believe that people with seniority possess more wisdom (Warburton, 2017b). Besides, in Nigerian enterprises, there is a clear ranking of employees and employers (Isado, 21 March 2018).

Initially, the leadership structure of Nigerians outlines the way in which the government is hierarchically ranked, according to the public office they occupy. To put it briefly, the Nigerian government has a lot of influence over companies and has the highest position of power and control within the country (Constitution of the Federal Republic of Nigeria, n.d.). Most commonly, Nigerian leaders are often addressed in the following three ways: *"Chief, managing director or executive director"* (CCBS Survey 2018). By mentioning the proper title, one acknowledges the leader's status. Despite hierarchy being present within the workforce, some organisations still have an open-door policy, meaning that people feel they can relate to their leaders and are comfortable seeking advice from them. Shirley Aipoh also notes that: *"You can have conversations with your boss, however, there is always that hierarchy, so it is not too free at the same time"* (Aipoh, 16 March 2018). So, although personal relationships are often maintained within a business, hierarchy is still present (CCBS Survey, 2018).

How Nigerians achieve leadership empathy

Belonging to a group is a very important aspect to Nigerians. Like in most African cultures, the country is seen to have a 'we' culture and for this reason, Nigerians will always be surrounded by people (Hofstede Insights, n.d.). Therefore, the relationship between a leader and the employees is of significance. In order to secure the best relationship, communication is key. Keeping this in mind, it is imperative for a leader to make use of indirect communication and to show politeness at all times. Additionally, the following three qualifications are essential to being a good leader: being warm, laid-back and having a good sense of humour (Lewis, 2006). Achieving empathy requires building upon those three qualifications. According to Lewis (2006), respecting others is another crucial aspect of achieving empathy for a Nigerian leader. Showing respect in the right manner and having knowledge of the Nigerian culture is needed. A foreign manager must constantly view things from a Nigerian cultural perspective. Patience is key since Nigerians do not like to rush. This calls for a flexible attitude towards employees. Employees will always expect a leader to accomplish what he or she promised. Lastly, a Nigerian leader will want to employ emotional intelligence (Okoye, 5 April 2018). As Oyoke states: *"Honesty, openness and trust are the catalysts to feel valued and to accomplish empathy as a leader"*.

Pakistan

Wakas Khawaja, Elisia Piperni, Nayaelah Siddiqui & Jenny Vuong

Pakistan (پاکستان(, a South Asian nation, is neighbour to the countries Iran, Afghanistan, China and India. Pakistan's southern coastline leads to the Arabian Sea. Although the country is relatively small in size, its population density is quite high. With approximately a quarter of the size of India's territory, Pakistan is the fifth most populated country in the world (Constable, 2017). The official language of Pakistan has recently been changed from English to Urdu in 2015. Interestingly, less than one-tenth of the country's population speaks Urdu while close to half of Pakistanis speak Punjabi (Khan, 2015). Several ethnic groups are part of Pakistan's population, including Punjabi, Sindhi, Pashtun and Baluchi (World Culture Encyclopaedia, n.d.).

Pakistan achieved its independence from British rule in 1947, making it a relatively young nation. The country is officially known as the Islamic Republic of Pakistan, and the vast majority of the population is Muslim (BBC, 2018). Its capital city is Islamabad. However, Karachi is its largest city and is known to be the country's business capital (Nations Online, n.d.). The country has experienced strong economic growth in recent years, and this is largely due to the strength of its construction sector along with the recovery of its agricultural sector (Ahmed, 2018). Additionally, there are plenty of opportunities in energy generation, information technology and infrastructure (Netherlands Enterprise Agency, n.d.). The Pakistani culture is rich and complex in both its history and current affairs, and the analysis below aims to provide some insight into its business environment and leaders.

How the Pakistanis characterise leaders

The leadership styles in Pakistan tend to be direct and task-oriented along with a focus on creating strong relationships that value trust (Mujtaba, Afza & Habib, 2011). Since Pakistan has a collectivist culture, employees value when leaders are directive about tasks and explain to them what and when something needs to be done. This behaviour by leaders reduces uncertainty for subordinates and provides more structure by defining responsibilities and roles.

Additionally, this further maintains the hierarchy in Pakistan, typified by predominantly centralised decision-making by leaders in high power positions, as will be discussed below (Hussain, Wan & Javed, 2017). Meanwhile, it is common and generally accepted for people with less power to not have a role in the decision-making process. Unlike Western societies where participative management is shown to make employees' performance thrive, in countries such as Pakistan, this sort of behaviour may be perceived as untrustworthy by the employers (Morris & Pavett, 1992). Furthermore, in such collectivist societies, leaders encourage individuals to view themselves as part of a collective and to work towards the collective interest of the group (Mujtaba et al., 2011). Moreover, because Pakistan has a high-context culture, non-verbal communication such as gestures, body language and facial expressions, is something to pay attention to (Lewis, 2006). Generally, similar to India, nepotism is quite common in Pakistan, whereby family members tend to work together and often the son is expected to take over the father's trade (Lewis, 2006).

Survey results and what local respondents say

Participants in the CCBS Survey (2018) indicate that Pakistanis value the relationship between their leaders and employees. As such, the clear majority either believe somewhat or completely that managers should actively spend time on the personal wellbeing of team members. However, as a project coordinator from Pakistan states, in larger corporations such as banks, leaders tend to remain less casual and intimate with their employees than leaders from smaller organisations (CCBS Survey, 2018).
In terms of leadership characteristics, employees expect their leader to be a powerful decision-maker and visionary thinker. They also admire leaders with great intellect, strong charismatic personality and the right family connections (CCBS Survey, 2018). In addition, Seema Arif, a Pakistani scholar, encourages leaders to listen to their employees to get to know them and to *"develop personal understanding and trust"* (Arif, 11 April 2018).

About gender equality, the majority of the respondents to the CCBS Survey insists that men and women do not have equal access to senior leadership positions. As Shaheen Akhtar, Chief Operating Officer of Path Limousine Services, states *"there are very few female leaders if you compare, but those that are there are very successful"* (Akhtar, 11 March 2018). This illustrates how women in Pakistan normally have limited opportunities to climb the ladder. Nevertheless, a few are able to do so very successfully. When asked about the differences between the leadership styles of men and women in Pakistan, a strong and clear presence of cultural influence was observed. Although Pakistan scores 50 on Hofstede's masculinity dimension (Hofstede Insights, n.d.), the CCBS Survey (2018) indicates that employees find it easier to listen to their male leaders and portray them as bold, practical and rational. Whilst, it seems it is harder for employees to listen to their female leaders as they are portrayed as being aggressive or making decisions based on emotions. As Pakistani programme manager Maleeha states, female leaders have to prove themselves at *"every forum and at every position due to our society and culture"* (CCBS Survey, 2018). Additionally, three-quarters of respondents indicate that employees cannot bend the rules without asking, even if it is done in order to improve their performance. Haroon Rashid Kanth, CEO and head of Teradata Delivery Center Pakistan, expresses that people are allowed *"to experiment within the defined parameters of values and culture to ensure consistency, but at the same time have high focus on creativity and innovation"* (CCBS Survey, 2018). Ali Semab, an engineering project manager, explains that it *"depends on the domain"*; areas that are foundational, *"such as safety, quality and stewardship"*, have rules that need to be *"strictly adhered to. In other areas, rules can be modified and innovation is rather encouraged"* (CCBS Survey, 2018).

Local leadership analysis

In-country literature review

Qaisar Abbas and Sara Yaqoob (2009) emphasise the importance of leadership development, which they state is something that impacts employee and organisational performance. Therefore, using the six leadership framework dimensions developed by Tirmizi, Abbas and Yaqoob explore the impact of leadership development in the business sector in Pakistan. Such training is currently trending in Pakistan as a means to develop human capital and the personal development of employees. Through their study, Abbas and Yaqoob found that the leadership dimensions affect performance 50 percent of the time. In particular, the dimension of coaching was used to solve problems among employees and inform them of expectations. Empowerment was used in specific ways to combat negativity and to increase job satisfaction. Participative decision-making was observed to make employees feel more competent at higher levels. However, a higher workload was noted as a leading factor that led to dissatisfaction. Delegation was also used to make employees more accountable and responsible. The other 50% of performance was contributed to factors such as attitude, commitment, motivation, trust in the organisation and rewards (Abbas & Yaqoob, 2009).

Another study (Tipu, Ryan & Fantazy, 2012) explores the impacts of transformational leadership, whereby a leader links a follower's self-concept with the company's mission and encourages loyalty to the organisational culture. The study indicates a positive correlation between the two. Additionally, it has found that organisational culture helps employees to innovate, accept and adopt new ideas within the organisation. Hence, it shows that the tone of the culture that top management establishes is crucial to an organisation.

Additionally, a third study by Danish and Usman (2010) looks at the factors that motivate employees and retain human capital. It was found that rewards, such as bonuses and recognition, have a strong impact on motivation. The following are all factors that scored higher on increasing employee motivation: promotional opportunities, positive relationships with co-workers, cooperation with supervisors and a secure job. Other factors, such as work content and difficulty of operating procedures, have a lesser impact on employee motivation.

Seema Arif: a Pakistani leadership scholar

Seema Arif is an associate professor at the School of Social Sciences and Humanities at the University of Management and Technology in Lahore. According to Seema Arif, leadership is *"about people and not tasks"* (Arif, 11 April 2018). She emphasises the importance of human development and of listening to employees in order to get to know them, which she believes leads to a *"better understanding"* and overall *"better performance"*.
When asked more specifically about Pakistani leadership, Arif finds that most Pakistani leaders are bureaucratic and practice a *"top to bottom, linear way of communication"*. In her experience, she often finds that power within the organisation is *"vested in upper ranks"*. In business, money tends to be a goal, whereas in politics, power and money are both considered more important than human development. Additionally, leaders usually want the employees to accomplish everything by themselves. The competition between employees is tough, and employees can easily get replaced (Arif, 11 April 2018).
Arif's views are in strong contrast to the respondents of the CCBS Survey (2018) but give an additional perspective on Pakistani leadership. Her perspective comes from being the head of department for seven years and setting up four departments in two universities. This shows that, although Pakistanis value

building relationships, misuse of the power at the top of the hierarchy deviates leaders from being more human-focused to money-focused and can make employees feel dissatisfied.

Shaheen Akhtar: a Pakistani cross-cultural trainer

Shaheen Akhtar is the Chief Operating Officer of Path Limousine Services, one of the largest transportation companies in Pakistan. According to Akhtar, leadership is encompassed by a person who has the ability to lead a team or a company towards their vision. The leader takes the employees to the next level (Akhtar, 11 March 2018). Akhtar (11 March 2018) mentions that culture always makes a difference in leadership style. He describes Pakistani leadership as direct, and that leaders fulfil their commitments. Furthermore, Akhtar explains that Pakistani leadership is relationship-based. Leaders care about their employees, which tends to make them more successful as a leader. For example, if an employee is in need of help, Akhtar would help them out personally. That makes the employees feel closer to him. In order to get a top position in a Pakistani company, you have to work your way up based on your ability and skills. "*You earn what you are capable of*" (Akhtar, 11 March 2018). But interestingly, Akhtar says that even in a top position in his company, a leader cannot make decisions on their own. When Akhtar makes decisions, he first discusses with his team. Thereafter, he brings it up with the board. In other words, all decisions are made collectively (Akhtar, 11 March 2018). This is in stark contrast to what the literature says, as will be explored below.

In-country leadership bestseller

Leadership Insights: Success Strategies from Pakistani Business Leaders Volume 2 is a locally written Pakistani book by Amer Qureshi and Qaiser Abbas. Qureshi is a professional with expertise in business, entrepreneurship and finance. He has many years of experience as a consultant and has worked with many CEOs, boards and management teams. His experience is rooted in multiple industries across numerous countries.

Abbas is an organisational psychologist, who is now a motivational speaker and success coach. He founded the Possibilities Foundation as well as the non-profit organisation, Youth Studio. He is very well-known around the world for his leadership teambuilding and coaching tools.

Title	Leadership Insights
Subtitle	Success Strategies from Pakistani Business Leaders
Author	Amer Qureshi and Qaiser Abbas
Publisher	Possibilities Publications
Year	2016
ISBN	9781365318757

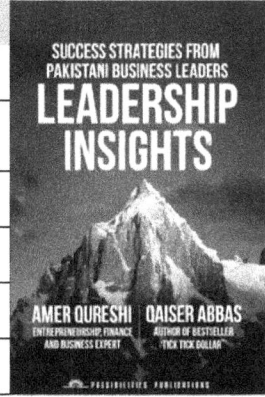

Through their collaborated book, Qureshi and Abbas aim to inform managers about what it takes to be successful as a leader in the Pakistani business environment specifically. While much leadership literature is Western-based, Qureshi and Abbas focus on the particularities of working in and running a business in the developing country of Pakistan. *Leadership Insights* has received a lot of praise from around the globe.

Pakistani leadership YouTube review

There are several experts with various views on how Pakistani leadership can be described, including what influences it and what it takes to be a good leader in the country. Because leadership is a topic that has only recently started to be discussed in Pakistan, the word can evoke other associations to Pakistanis than it does in Western countries. Qasim Ali Shah explains that the problem in Pakistan is that leadership, just like communication skills and vision, are not covered thoroughly enough in the educational systems in the country. This of course results in a lack of good leaders. He believes it is very important to teach about leadership (Qasim Ali Shah, 2015). Ali Shah points out that because leadership is not taught in school, Pakistanis often do not know some of the basics of leadership, such as the complete definition of a leader, how a leader should perform and what the outcomes of being a leader could be. Therefore, it is difficult for a Pakistani to judge leadership on itself (Qasim Ali Shah, 2015).

In addition, Saad Hamid (2018) asserts that it is wrong for Pakistanis to think that they can learn from world's top leaders who often come from Western societies and, therefore, are unaware of the problems that take place in a Pakistani household. He emphasises the importance of developing a local leadership model that works particularly for Pakistanis, rather than looking at leadership models used in other countries (Hamid, 2018).

Understanding hierarchy in Pakistan

In the Pakistani culture, the path to a good understanding of hierarchy in the workplace can begin by looking at the Hofstede dimension of power distance. Pakistan ranks intermediately in power distance, with a score of 55. Seeing as this score is quite an intermediate ranking, the nation's preferences lean toward neither extreme of the dimension (Hofstede Insights, n.d.). However, it does mean that hierarchy exists to some significant degree in Pakistani culture (otherwise the score would be much lower). The analysis below provides some insight into this fact. According to a Pakistani local's perspective shared with Global Affairs Canada (2017), decision-making in the general Pakistani business environment mainly sits with top management. This is particularly true of the public sector and governmental departments, where the bosses are the ultimate decision makers with little to no input from employees. In the private sector, supervisors remain the final decision makers as well. However, the decision-making process within the private sector is more inclusive and participatory, where employees tend to feel more comfortable approaching management with new ideas (Global Affairs Canada, 2017).

Interactions and relations between employees and their supervisors tend to be formal. Nevertheless, while business leaders in Pakistan are more or less autocratic in decision-making, as stated above, they are also said to possess a certain degree of paternalism towards their subordinates (Commisceo Global, n.d.). This means that business leaders take a small interest in employees beyond the professional setting, and that employees are enabled to approach their superiors with more personal issues. This fact is supported by Qureshi and Abbas (2016) as well, who state that leaders should not simply engage their team on a professional level but also on an emotional level. This is crucial for a leader who wishes to build a top-performing, successful team in the workplace. This is even further supported by the CCBS Survey question mentioned above where most Pakistanis respondents agree that managers should invest in their employees

(2018). However, it is important that a leader understands that loss of respect is a likely result of attempting to befriend employees or act as a peer to them (Commisceo Global, n.d.). Hierarchy in the Pakistani business world is a rather delicate balance, where leaders must take control and have the utmost authority but also must be receptive to building more of a familial tie in their relationships with their employees.

How Pakistanis achieve leadership empathy

In Pakistan, people show empathy for moral and cultural reasons. Showing empathy is part of the nation's culture, but this is also reflected in business (Mughal, 17 February 2018). A leader in Pakistan can achieve empathy by being humanistic and offering promotions to the employees. Respect, warmth and zest are also highly valued amongst Pakistanis. Showing respect and offering good business is the key to building a relationship with a Pakistani in a professional environment. Pakistanis appreciate follow-up. Therefore, it is appreciated if a leader communicates often and clearly. Most of the time, a leader in Pakistan can attract good attention by being courteous and imaginative towards others. When employees are facing difficulties, a leader can motivate them by showing empathy and sympathy (Lewis, 2006). Moreover, Naveed Nasir Mughal (17 February 2018), a business expert in Islamabad, emphasises the importance of showing support to employees. By demonstrating and offering them support, employees tend to feel more encouraged and comfortable in the workplace. A loyal employee that has been working for a long time will get support from the employer when in need. According to Mughal (17 February 2018), Pakistani leaders put their employees first. This is supported further by Seema Arif, who has herself *"practiced empathetic leadership"*. For Arif, empathetic leadership includes *"coaching, guiding and counselling [employees] to focus on their personal skills...and become valuable professionals"* (Arif, 11 April 2018).

Philippines

Samuël Boerhoop, Patrick Dell & Robbert Pieete

In the South China Sea, between China, Vietnam and Indonesia, lies an island group that is one of the most diverse countries in terms of ethnicity: the Philippines. The Philippines consists of more than seven thousand islands, although the eleven largest islands account for the vast majority of the total population and size (Moran, Harris & Moran, 2011). The main language spoken in the country is Filipino. English is also widely spoken and is the second language of the country. Apart from Filipino and English, there are more than 150 languages spoken in the Philippines (Global Affairs Canada, 2017). The reason for the multiculturalism of the country is the immigration of other nations in the past. Starting with the Spanish settlement four centuries ago, followed by the occupation of the British, the Japanese and the Americans, the immigrants enriched Filipino culture considerably (Moran et al., 2011). *"Throughout history, Filipinos are known to be adaptable, flexible, friendly, creative and resilient. We easily adjust to various cultures and situations. This is also one reason why millions of Filipinos are contracted to work abroad as Overseas Filipino Workers (OFWs)"* (Marquez, 9 April 2018). Due to the American influence, the education system is well-established and also free through secondary school, resulting in almost all Filipinos being highly literate (Moran, Harris & Moran, 2011).
With the majority of its inhabitants being Roman Catholic, the Philippines is the largest Catholic country in Asia (Schweitzer & Alexander, 2015). The country's economy relies mainly on agriculture, forestry and fishing. These sectors account for more than half of the country's export and labour market (Moran et al., 2011). The four biggest trading partners are China, USA, Japan and the EU. Fuel and machinery are the most common import products (Moran et al., 2011; Incallado, 9 April 2018).

How the Filipinos characterise leaders

Leadership in the Philippines has a strong relational aspect to it. Filipino leaders are often expected to adopt a parental role, which involves giving clear directives and discipline but is also accompanied by the type of personal obligations expected from a familial relationship (Globe, n.d.). This statement is supported by Castillo-Carandang, who stated in an interview that: *"a successful Philippine leader is one who listens, one who shows that he cares. The personal relationships are also important for a successful Filipino leader"* (Castillo-Carandang, 21 March 2018). CCBS Survey findings (2018) show similar results on a comparable survey question. A large majority of the respondents agree that a manager should actively spend time on the personal wellbeing of the team members. Besides showing genuine interest in the private lives of subordinates, it is important for leaders to behave like a parent to them. *"A successful Filipino leader for me is somebody who takes people under his or her wing. Giving them the chance to grow, coaching them, mentoring them"* (Castillo-Carandang, 21 March 2018). Besides that, none of the respondents could relate themselves to the statement that leaders prefer to keep a personal distance from employees to maintain the right level of respect (CCBS Survey, 2018). Like Castillo-Carandang (21 March 2018) explains, *"subordinates would like to see the leader as a friend also, a leader who will not leave them behind when times are rough"*.

Filipinos are often described as emotional people and are, therefore, very sensitive to receiving feedback. This aspect applies to both social and business situations, according to Moran, Harris and Moran (2011). A leader who wants to be successful in the Philippines should, therefore, be very cautious with giving feedback to subordinates. According to the CCBS Survey (2018), Filipinos prefer to hear criticism in an indirect manner and outside staff meetings. Castillo-Carandang (21 March 2018) agrees: *"If you give them (Filipinos) feedback, it has to be delivered in a very gentle manner also reinforced with the feeling of sincerity"*. Furthermore, there are a few other aspects which need to be taken into consideration by foreigners when working in the Philippines. Respondents to the CCBS Survey (2018) clearly indicate that when a decision is made by the management, it is not common for it to be doubted or changed. Finally, Filipinos are unwilling to do business with others, unless interpersonal sincerity is present. Moran, Harris and Moran (2011) suggest that this has been one of the biggest obstacles between Filipinos and Americans, as Americans are perceived to be overly aggressive and insensitive.

Survey results and what local respondents say

In the CCBS Survey, local participants were asked how they identify a good leader. The majority of the participants claims that a leader should have organisational experience and technical competence. If a leader is capable, he or she will be looked-up to by his or her subordinates. Additionally, the survey respondents indicate that a leader should be a powerful decision maker, a visionary thinker and a good listener (CCBS Survey, 2018). As Castillo-Carandang (21 March 2018) confirms, a leader must take care of his or her subordinates. Furthermore, it is important for a leader to be intellectual, resourceful and possess a strong charismatic personality (CCBS Survey, 2018).

The best time to plan a meeting in the Philippines is between 9 am and 10 am, according to more than half of the survey respondents. The meetings should preferably be held in the office itself (CCBS Survey, 2018). Furthermore, you should be on time because, in the Philippines, deadlines must be met at all times. The vast majority of the survey respondents believes that missing a deadline counts more or less as a failure (CCBS Survey, 2018).

As stated in the introduction, the Philippines is a culturally diverse country. The reason for this, according to Rey Elbo, a business columnist, is that *"[t]he Philippines has been colonized by Spain and the United States and occupied by Japan during WWII. We are heavily influenced by Spain's Catholicism and the American way of life that many of us speak good English. They also influenced our leadership style that even up to these days, we rely on American textbooks to educate ourselves"* (CCBS Survey, 2018). A Filipino professor and former AVP Director agrees that the country's leadership is a *"blending of [a] Western and Asian brand of leadership"* (CCBS Survey, 2018).

Furthermore, more than half of the participants agree that bending rules without asking is common. However, most of the participants believe that situations are not always black and white and that there are exceptions. As Marquez (9 April 2018), cultural entrepreneur, argues: *"It really depends on the situation. We follow standard procedures to have a smoother workflow but as times evolve and there are certain situations that are unique, we exercise common sense and adaptability"*. Incallado (9 April 2018), a manager, expresses that management should always be informed of such happenings, *"...especially if it's not according to our rules, and beyond our acceptable standards"*.

Local leadership analysis

In-country literature review

In 2013, Filipino columnist Regina Galang Reyes wrote an article in a local newspaper entitled "Developing a Filipino brand of leadership". In it, she notes that Filipinos are often trained in Western theories of management and leadership and poses the question whether these theories are applicable within the context of Filipino culture (Reyes, 2013). A study was conducted from 1993 to 1999 involving middle management and organisations from various businesses in 62 countries. According to Jean-Pierre Segal, director at Université Paris-Dauphine: *"A management approach adapted to the local norms of living and working together must be applied"* (Segal, 2012). During the 2012 conference in the Ateneo of Manila University, on "The Role of Culture in Effective Leadership", Reyes (2013) noted that this principle is often overlooked in the Philippines and that many Filipino leaders are disconnected from their local context and the need for their leadership and leadership development to be culturally specific. Within the article, Bienvenido F. Nebres, S.J., former president of Ateneo de Manila, explains that Filipino leaders basically have to operate within two conflicting cultures, namely the native culture and the Western culture. He notes that the latter currently overrides the native culture in the Philippines. Nebres also thinks that this results in *"dysfunctional behavior and paralysis in execution"* among Filipino leaders (as cited in Reyes, 2013). According to Nebres, it is up to Filipinos to challenge the existing concepts of leadership as many of the Western scenarios on leadership do not apply to their country. He therefore cautioned Filipinos not to apply Western leadership models uncritically as the failure of such models in a Philippine context will still lead to the person who applied them being blamed (Reyes, 2013). In his opinion, Filipino leaders need to discover what makes for effective leadership within the own culture and context (Reyes, 2013).

Martin Aguilar: a Filipino leadership scholar

Martin Aguilar (27 March 2018) is the founder and lead consultant of The Filipino Hospitality. He has fifteen years of industry experience in hospitality. He shared that his previous colleagues in the hotels and resorts he used to manage would describe him as *"a servant leader"*. In explanation of how this came about, Aguilar quotes one of his mentors: *"Before you could command you must first learn how to obey and before you could lead you must first learn how to follow"* (Aguilar, 27 March 2018).

When questioned what is considered good leadership in the Philippines, Aguilar answers: *"We, as a very social people, think good leaders are viewed to be someone who knows how to balance things. You cannot have all work and no play so you need to be someone they can relate to, someone they can also converse with"* (Aguilar, 27 March 2018). In the relationship between a leader and a subordinate, Filipinos will go beyond the line of just being social with each other. Aguilar (27 March 2018) acknowledges: *"Sometimes bosses or leaders would be like the godparent of someone in marriage. … That is somewhat typical in our culture".* Although this may be typical in Filipino culture, Aguilar mentions that one of his mentors taught him that it is sometimes better to draw a social line. When a connection between a leader and subordinate gets too personal, Aguilar explains: *"If for example someone like a subordinate would have that sort of connection, a closer connection as compared to others, I think the expectation is higher"* (Aguilar, 27 March 2018). Aguilar (27 March 2018) further explains how leaders show their emotions in their working environment. He recognises that it is not possible to ignore emotions at all times. Leaders can get tired, angry and disappointed. As Filipinos are described as emotional people, Aguilar concludes: *"I think it is really a matter of trying to control these emotions, trying to still focus on the end goals"* (Aguilar, 27 March 2018). Because Filipinos are emotional people, the communication style is very indirect, according to Aguilar (27 March 2018). In order to send a message without hurting the feelings of subordinates, he suggests: *"Within providing comments we would often find ourselves using the sandwich method, where we start with a positive attribute, before we can proceed with areas of improvement and then end off with a positive comment again"* (Aguilar, 27 March 2018).

Finally, Aguilar explains what is meant by "Filipino time". This is a negative attribute ascribed to Filipinos. He illustrates that when traffic is busy, a short distance of 20 minutes can take more than three hours. Although he admits that it is never an excuse, it can really be erratic at times. He concludes *"So, that is quite a common notion wherein the Filipino time is quite delayed, where most of our schedules are often affected with a lot of reasons"* (Aguilar, 27 March 2018).

Nina Castillo-Carandang: a Filipino cross-cultural trainer

Nina Castillo-Carandang is a Filipino scholar who introduces herself as follows: *"I have an academic background in sociology, clinical epidemiology and global health. I'm a faculty member of the Department of Clinical Epidemiology, College of Medicine [at the] University of the Philippines, Manila"* (Castillo-Carandang, 21 March 2018). According to her LinkedIn-profile, she has sixteen years of experience as a Cross-Cultural Consultant (Nina Castillo-Carandang, n.d).

When discussing what being a good Filipino leader means, Castillo-Carandang answers: *"A successful Filipino leader for me is somebody who takes people under their wing. Giving them a chance to grow, coaching them, mentoring them. That would be an ideal Filipino leader"* (Castillo-Carandang, 21 March 2018).
A relationship between a leader and his or her subordinates is also very important: *"The relationship is always two ways around. You cannot just expect*

the subordinates to adapt to the leader without the leader also adapting the other way. It is a mutual relationship. Both of them need to exert effort to understand each other, to be able to listen well to each other and also have a good sense of what is working well and what is not working well" (Castillo-Carandang, 21 March 2018). Whether a leader is from the Philippines or from a foreign country is irrelevant according to Castillo-Carandang (21 March 2018): "If the Filipino manager is just as competent as the foreign manager, then most colleagues would look up to both of them. But if either the foreign manager or the Filipino manager [is] incompetent or perceived as uncaring then I don't think it makes a difference if you are a Philippine or foreigner".

In-country leadership bestseller

The book *Leadership That Matters,* written by Francis J. Kong in 2017, is one of the Philippine bestsellers regarding leadership. Kong is an inspirational public speaker, leadership consultant and a columnist. His book motivates and develops the right character and discipline to grow as a good leader.

Local leadership book		
Title	Leadership That Matters	
Subtitle	-	
Author	Francis J. Kong	
Publisher	ABS-CBN Publishing	
Year	2017	
ISBN	978-971-816-194-4	

Kong describes his book as *"... a collection of short articles that cover leadership issues intended to provide tools and ideas for leaders to use in the midst of the fast-changing business landscape. The approach is highly inspirational, and its anecdotal treatment makes it universally relevant"* (Kong, 6 March 2018).

Philippines leadership YouTube review

One of the most prevalent subjects regarding leadership in the Philippines that is found on YouTube is the call for gender equality. This indicates that there is still a gender gap between Filipino workers. During an interview on CNN Philippines, Former President of CAMPI, Elisabeth H. Lee, gave her opinion on being a female CEO: *"Being a woman in a male-dominated industry can be positive, because you naturally stick out, and the difference is that women have more empathy, but in the end, results matter!"* (Lee, 2018).

Understanding hierarchy in the Philippines

Just like in other Asian countries, hierarchy is present in Filipino businesses. However, the amount of power someone has is not influenced by his or her age or class. Instead, as mentioned by Schweitzer and Alexander (2015), a person's status can change depending on his or her track record or the garnering of people's trust. Aguilar (27 March 2018) acknowledges the presence of hierarchy in the Philippines: *"Someone of the front office staff, if he or she has a concern, cannot go directly to see the general manager or the CEO"*. An anonymous survey respondent notes that hierarchy at times has a negative effect in Philippine companies: *"In the Philippine culture, 'hierarchy' is respected and people are so bound to give due respect to those in position. Sometimes, it is good, though in many cases, it does not encourage collaboration as the leader could dominate discussions and others do not bother to listen to the team members at all"* (CCBS Survey, 2018). Since there is a power distance between the leaders and their subordinates, it is important to use titles suited to the positions of the leader when addressing them, according to CCBS Survey (2018). This title and position is important for a leader to have, and as Schweitzer and Alexander (2015) confirms, should be mentioned on a business card as well. This opinion is also supported by the majority of the participants in the CCBS Survey (2018). Therefore, it is not surprising that subordinates should not address their leader by merely his or her first name, as this is seen as disrespectful. However, an anonymous respondent of the CCBS Survey (2018) disagrees: *"Yes, probably, we can, but I haven't found anyone calling their managers by [their] first name. As a sign of respect, we use Ma'am or Sir to address our managers"*.

Castillo-Carandang (21 March 2018) agrees that addressing a leader on a first-name basis is a sign of disrespect. *"I always say, please allow us the chance to be respectful, because that is very much part of our culture"*. Yet, she also claims that it might be possible that after a while, a leader will be called Sir or Mister, followed by his or her first name in front of it, or a leader could even be called by his or her nickname. Although there is a difference between hierarchical layers in the Philippines, the difference between men and women in the business world is very small. In fact, almost all of the participants of the CCBS Survey (2018) believe that men and women have equal access to senior leadership positions. Dr José Florencio F. Lapeña, Jr., a professor and university scientist, confirms this: *"We have had two woman-presidents of the country, and many 'tough' CEOs, COOs, CIOs. We (men) have no problem deferring to a female boss"* (CCBS Survey, 2018). Moran, Harris and Moran (2011) even emphasise that the Philippines is proud to be one of the few Asian countries that have a relatively large percentage of women in government.

How the Philippines achieve leadership empathy

In the Philippines, the contact between leaders and their subordinates revolves around harmony. Therefore, according to Culture Crossing Guide (n.d.), conflict and confrontation should be avoided. Lewis (2006) emphasises that modesty, gentleness and courtesy are traits expected by Filipinos. When criticising someone, it is done subtly and in combination with praising other things (Lewis, 2006). In addition, as Moran, Harris and Moran (2011) indicate, someone is never criticised in public or with others around as this feels embarrassing to the person being criticised and therefore is greatly insulting. Castillo-Carandang (21 March 2018) confirms this statement: *"If you give them feedback, it has to be delivered in a very gentle manner, also reinforced with the feeling of sincerity"*. Relationships are also crucial in the Filipino business world. Close personal relations are important and for a leader to be liked, as Lewis (2006) also mentions. Castillo-Carandang (21 March 2018) acknowledges this: *"It is not just business, it is not just office work which is important, it is the personal relationships that you build along the way"*. A leader should support his or her subordinates in rough times and stand up for them, even if it damages his or her own reputation. Socialising is also important for a leader in building a relationship with his or her subordinates: *"Go and eat a snack or lunch or dinner and go and spend some time in karaoke. Go and attend the birthday parties or the weddings that you might be invited to"* (Castillo-Carandang, 21 March 2018). Aguilar (27 March 2018) agrees with this idea by mentioning that a good leader communicates often with his or her staff.

Portugal

Bob Driesen, Charlotte ten Berge & Jesse Gerritsen

Portugal is located on the Iberian Peninsula in south-western Europe. Spain is its only neighbouring country, leaving the remaining borders of the republic surrounded by the North Atlantic Ocean. Portugal has a maritime character, with two island groups belonging to it: Madeira and the Azores. The city of Lisbon is the capital and largest city of the country. Portugal is home to approximately 11 million citizens. The most commonly spoken language is Portuguese, followed by French. Approximately 20 percent of the people also speak English, mostly in the big cities and tourist areas. Portugal is one of the warmest European countries, with a mild Mediterranean climate. The country is well-known for its delicious cuisine. Among the many Portuguese specialities, *pastel de nata's* and *cataplana de marisco* stand out with their exquisite taste.

How the Portuguese characterise leaders

The most important leadership attributes, identified by GLOBE in Portugal are integrity, decisiveness, team integration and being inspirational and performance-orientated. This information is congruent with the findings of the CCBS Survey (2018), in which Portuguese respondents indicate that they expect from their leaders to be powerful decision-makers, good listeners and visionary thinkers. This is also emphasised by José Laborinho, a Portuguese business manager. He states that: *"employees expect from their manager to be a decision maker and to make the final decision"* (Laborinho, 20 March 2018). For Portuguese employees, it is essential that their *chefe* (boss) has a strong charismatic personality and access to the right networks. Furthermore, employees look up to a leader who possesses technical competence and organisational experience (CCBS Survey, 2018). Moreover, as stated in the GLOBE visualisation scales, Portuguese leaders are charismatic, team-oriented and participative (Globe, n.d.). Frank Weermeijer, a business professional in Portugal explains in an interview with CCBS that: *"the ones who are led usually do not give any feedback, they just accept the instructions"* (CCBS Survey, 2018).

According to the CCBS Survey (2018) results, only a small part of the respondents admit to being independent when it comes to following the established procedures of an organisation. The majority indicate that they would never bend the rules without asking, even if it means achieving better results (CCBS Survey, 2018). This is also pointed out by Frank Weermeijer, who says: *"Portuguese leaders are very hierarchical, they tend to lead by instruction".* He concludes his interview by stating: *"Portuguese leadership is distant"* (CCBS Survey, 2018).

Survey results and what local respondents say

The CCBS survey has gathered insight from over sixty Portuguese professionals who shared their knowledge and experience on leadership in Portugal. The most significant results of this survey can be summarised as follows: firstly, three-quarter of the professionals agree with the statement that missing a deadline is more or less the same as failure. Secondly, a larger number of Portuguese professionals answers that when a management decision has been made, it will not be changed very easily. This statement supports the theory of Hofstede that Portugal scores high on the power distance scale, meaning leaders carry a lot of power in the Portuguese business world (Hofstede Insights, n.d.). In addition to that, over three-quarters of the respondents indicate that employees may not bend the rules to improve their performance or achieve better results. A Portuguese marketing manager elaborates by saying: *"There are some guidelines that can't be broken: health and safety, business principles, ethics and compliance. Everything else is open for challenge"* (CBSS Survey, 2018). Lastly, Portuguese professionals consider the most typical Portuguese leadership terms to be teamwork, directness regarding communications towards each other and low-profile keeping. As one of the respondents illustrates: *"In my organization we try to act like a team. Employees follow the leadership without problems and no authoritarian attitudes are required"* (CCBS Survey, 2018).

Local leadership analysis

In-country literature review

Luís Sítima is a professor at the Porto Business School, where he is responsible for the coordination of the Global Advanced Leadership Program. He is the writer of *LEADERS Handbook: A Mudança Começa e Acaba nas Pessoas*, which means: change begins and ends with human beings. The book is a guide for individual development and meant for everybody that wants to make a difference in any diverging context. The book is written in a creative way, offering the reader a unique individual development experience. Sítima (2016) combines theoretical concepts with countless personal success stories and experiences, which makes it an exciting technical book to read.

In-country leadership bestseller

One of the best-selling books on leadership is written by Armenio Rego and Miguel Pina e Cuncha, published in 2003. *A Essência de Liderança*, which is Portuguese for the essence of leadership.

Local leadership book	
Title	A Essência de Liderança
Subtitle	Mudança - Resultados - Integridade
Author	Armenio Rego & Miguel Pina e Cunha
Publisher	Editora RH
Year	2007
ISBN	9789728853013

In the book, important tips on effective leadership in Portugal are given. It also looks at what characterises a leader and argues that without a substantial and active following, Portuguese leaders cannot drive change (Fnac, 2018). Other captivating stories are told by Armenio Rego, Portuguese writer and professor with more than 300 research items. He has written a lot of books on leadership in Portugal in an interesting, yet evidence-based style (Arménio Rego, 2018).

Portuguese leadership YouTube review

LUHDICA is a YouTube channel, which educates professionals on becoming a leader. The creator explains what kind of leadership to use in different situations. For example, he often mentions the term situational leadership. Moreover, examples are given on how to deal with the challenges of short-term goals. In those situations, he notes that it is imperative to be more autocratic towards your followers (LUHDICA, 2015).

Another video worth mentioning is from a conference with Armenio Rego, where he speaks about his new book: *As Lições de Liderança* (leadership lessons). The book pays attention to a leader's body language and how it aids managers. According to Rego (2015), speaking is only 20 percent of communication, leaving the other 80 percent to body language.

Understanding hierarchy in Portugal

As the survey reveals, a large majority of the Portuguese respondents does not keep a personal distance from their employers, in order to maintain the right level of respect and hierarchy (CCBS Survey, 2018). This is in conflict with Hofstede's Power Index (Hofstede, 2005). The Power Index shows a score of 63, which is quite high, meaning that inequality is largely accepted within the country. In other words, the more power one person has, the more privileges a person is prone to receive. Furthermore, this theory states that there is a big variance regarding salary between the top and the base of an organisation. This contrasts with the majority of the CCBS Survey (2018) results. Only a quarter of the Portuguese leaders agree with the fact that within their organisation a leader gets respectable office space and transportation, as to match the position. This statement is different from the theory of Hofstede's Power Index (Hofstede, 2005). However, this could be confirmed by the theory of Trompenaars, which reveals that collectivism is equal to propinquity. That explains why leaders in Portugal would not feel pleased with having a large office space in comparison with other employees. Despite living in a hierarchical country, personnel in Portugal are not required to address their leaders by their titles or positions. In fact, based on the survey results more than half of the employees can call their leader by his or her first name (CCBS Survey, 2018). However, a professional argues: *"It really depends on the area you work in. Banking and law are very formal, marketing and advertising not at all"* (CCBS Survey, 2018). Then again, Hofstede's theory about high power distance states the opposite. However, this may be caused by the fact that leaders in Portugal prefer to have a more personal relationship with their teams.

How the Portuguese achieve leadership empathy

Portuguese culture is one of giving. It is normal within a company to exchange gifts with other colleagues. So, always make sure you have a present from your company or country. That is one way, in which a leader can try to achieve empathy. During business trips, it is customary for the host to take you to dinner. By getting to know you and your family, a Portuguese person decides whether you are fit for doing business. Personal relationships are key, as well as mutual confidence. A client in Portugal will be seen as a friend, if that is not the case, then you might lose the client. José Laborinho notes in the interview: *"As a leader, you also need to make your employees feel more important"* (Laborinho, 20 March 2018). With this statement, he implies that there is a need to make employees feel valued within the company. That makes them feel special and therefore achieves empathy. Relationships in Portugal begin with an open mind and assume trust. What is more, though feedback is not communicated directly, face-to-face communication is important for achieving empathy with other parties (Lewis & Gates, 2005). According to the survey, more than forty percent of Portuguese employees expect their leader to be a good listener. Around 80 percent of the professionals answer that it is wise for a manager to actively spend time on the well-being of the employees. On the question, what makes leadership in your country unique, a Portuguese professional answers, that it is normal in Portugal that *"People talk a lot about their lives, even with their superiors"* (CCBS Survey, 2018). More than 60 percent of the leaders do not see keeping personal distance from their employees as important.

Saudi Arabia

Dominique Gunnink, Alexander Dewell & Geraldine van Dillewijn

Boasting the largest landmass in the Gulf region (almost six times bigger than Germany), Saudi Arabia borders a number of countries, including Yemen, Bahrain, Oman, UAE, Qatar, Iraq, Jordan and Kuwait. Having a population a third of that of France, it is surprising that a third of Saudi Arabia's population is made up by non-nationals. Saudi Arabia has been predominantly Bedouin, meaning that tribal identity is key for the families. Being the home of Mecca, Saudi Arabia is central to the Sunni Muslim faith and gains a lot of religious tourism due to Hajj (pilgrimage). Saudi Arabia has the largest oil fields in the world, which historically were defended against the UAE and Qatar. Due to this, Saudi Arabia is of great importance for foreign trade, which has catapulted the population to the twelfth richest in the world (McMullan, 2018). Saudi Arabia has a rising young population with just over a quarter of the population being younger than fourteen. Saudi Arabia has a vast royal family, which is said to trace their lineage back to Mohammed. Unlike Western royal lines, Arabic hereditary lines are horizontal (from brother to brother) rather than vertical (from father to son). Saudi Arabia is organised through the Hijri (Islamic) calendar rather than the Gregorian calendar. The Hijri is a lunar calendar that emphasises holy months, such as Ramadan, which requires daylight fasting, which is enforced by the law. The resting day is Saturday, with the first day of the week being Sunday. The King (Salman Al Saud) and the heir (Mohammad bin Salman) have been Westernising Saudi Arabia in recent years by allowing women to drive and by combing through the government for corrupt officials.

How the Saudis characterise leaders

Saudi Arabia characterises their leaders in a traditional way. Having a large sense of hierarchy due to a late tribal heritage, Saudis seek an all-encompassing leader who is *"[s]trong when necessary, especially when it comes to defending or requesting support from management"* (CCBS Survey, 2018). Current Saudi leaders are generally more globally aware, smart, tech-savvy and typically have greater access to higher education (Al-Jibreen, 2014). A leader should be one that can answer a difficult question without hesitation and can have a solution to every problem either imminent or in the long-run. Although a Saudi leader should have a council of knowledgeable experts to advise in private, in public it should seem as if he or she is all knowing. As Saudi Arabia is a patriarchal society, many Saudis will characterise a leader as a man, even though female CEO numbers are rising every year. Saudi women are mainly employed in government and in the private education sector (Achoui, 2009). Due to Saudi Arabia's nomadic nature, it holds a lot of similarities to its Gulf neighbours. While the tribes are very different to the Omani and Qatari tribes, the ideals are similar due to environmental and religious connections.

Survey results and what local respondents say

Saudis feel strongly that missing a deadline is more or less the same as a failure as almost half of the respondents of the CCBS Survey (2018) state that they agree with the statement. Just over half of the respondents agree that a manager should actively spend more time on the personal well-being of the team members, with a third strongly agreeing. Physical connections are normal for management as it is a way to connect on a deeper level, as confirmed by Dr Sami A. Khan *"Saudis are known for that, Creating nice work, more hugging each other and kissing each other "* (Khan, 28 March 2018). Saudi managers seem to encourage competition to receive good results as nearly half of the respondents express that they have witnessed this in the workplace. A local general manager, Mohammed S. Alsaif, remarks that *"women tend to be more competitive due to cultural pressure on women working"* (CCBS Survey, 2018).

Half of the respondents agree or strongly agree that leaders get office space and benefits that are determined by their title. With leadership comes sole decision-making as there is a fear of consulting management that leaders deem beneath them *"The leader avoids [consulting] other levels of management in decision making"* (CCBS Survey, 2018). Three-quarters of the respondents confirm that academic titles are important to state either in the form of a business card or by including it in an email. An important title to keep an eye out for is *"الرئيس التنفيذي"* as it translates into CEO.

Local leadership analysis

In-country literature review: Al-Jibreen

Saudi Arabia has gone through a rapid cultural shift from a tribal state to a leading global exporter. This shift has led to an evolution of generations and their characteristics. Saudi national, Hamad Al-Jibreen (2014), has written an in-depth timeline about how the mindset of a Saudi has changed from pre-oil (1938) to the current generation. With tribal ties comes a close-knit community, helping those in need and having a humble mindset. This transformed through the oil generation in which the majority of the ministries were created as they began to drop their community bonds and began to view the collection of tribes as a unified country (Al-Jibreen, 2014). In the late 1980s, a new generation began seeing an increase in the number of expats coming to work in Saudi Arabia. However, this generation also had high positions that were readily available for Saudis when they entered the workforce, which Al-Jibreen argues led to a generation that was narcissistic because they were raised during a time of luxury. This generation of leaders are also, he argues, typically technologically impaired and reluctant to change (Al-Jibreen, 2014). With this, however, came loyalty to their company, and it became relationship-focused. It is important to mention that this was the time when Saudis had management roles. Since then, Saudi Arabia has worked hard to successfully change the work ethic of employees to ones that are leadership-oriented, open-minded, globally aware, fast and good at multitasking (Al-Jibreen, 2014).

Dr Sami A. Khan: a Saudi leadership scholar

Dr Sami A. Kahn (29 March 2018) is a professor in human resource management at King Abdulaziz University in Jeddah. Khan shared interesting insights into management styles within Saudi Arabia during an interview. He distinguishes between multinational companies that are highly organised and small to medium enterprises and family run companies that still operates by the top-down approach. Kahn explains that Saudi Arabia is a still a very collectivistic society and this extends into the workplace environment. Therefore, relationships, connections and networks are very important. He further emphasises that Saudis are still straight-forward people who believe in relationships to advance businesses. Trust is key to all of this, which is unlike companies in the West. For Saudis, trust leads to a long-term orientated business which is important for the future synergy of assets (Khan, 29 March 2018).

In-country leadership bestseller

One of the best-selling books about leadership was edited by Rajasekar and Beh , entitled *Culture and Gender in Leadership*. It shows the differences in gender leadership between the Middle East and Asia, highlighting ⁻ᵃ ˇ differences but also some stark similarities. Two of the contributing authors, Khan and Varshney (2013), argue that a Middle Eastern leader should be a transformational leader who can find obtainable solutions to business concerns and is capable of influencing others to achieve greater goals. Khan and Varshney (2013) patch together literature from both regions, creating a concise and knowledgeable argument. Leaders should have a future plan and always be one step ahead by anticipating future likelihoods for which they should plan alternative strategies to meet uncertainties. Khan and Varshney explain how leaders need to be sociable creatures who are able to explain their thoughts and plans and *listen, consult and involve others with self-confidence and must be able to* (Khan & Varshney, 2013).

Local leadership book		
Title	**Culture and Gender in Leadership**	
Author	Transformational Leadership in the Saudi Arabian Cultural Context: Prospects and Challenges	
Publisher	Sami A. Khan	
Year	Palgrave Macmillan	
ISBN	2015	

YouTube review: The Saudi-UK Business Forum Review

The Saudi Arabian business forum took the opportunity to discuss the increasing opportunities for women in leadership roles. Some topics raised include: how to encourage female participation, challenges facing female entrepreneurs and the quotas that are being implemented to try and increase the number of females in leadership or board positions. The panel of women that were discussing women in leadership included the President of the Federation for Community Sports in Saudi Arabia, Princess Reema bint Bandar; Saudi Deputy Minister of Labour and Social Development, Tamader Al-Rammah; Dr Basma Saleh Al-Buhairan; CEO of Samba Financial Group, Rania Nashar; and Executive Manager of Misk

Innovation, Deemah Alyahya. To further discuss the topic regarding quotas for placing women into leadership positions, the panel was asked whether you should focus on these targets for placing women in such positions or should you ignore them? An argument that is made is that it should really be the best person fitting that position and someone who can add value rather than just placing a woman there to reach the quota. However, there should be no obstacles in the way that should stop women from being able to reach these positions, and at the moment, the convention of the desert is still prevalent and cause discrimination against women. Saudi Arabian Princess, Reema bint Bandar, notes that instead of having these quotas it would be more efficient to create all of the necessary training which would allow for equal competition *"allow everyone the equal opportunity to have the skills and then they can compete on an equal level. Then women can demonstrate and prove that we can do better but equally"* (CIC Saudi Arabia, 2018). The Saudi Arabian government are starting to provide more initiatives to help and support women into leadership roles.

Understanding hierarchy in Saudi Arabia

Hierarchy is a cultural cornerstone in both Saudi Arabia's history and lifestyle. Unlike the flat hierarchy of Europe and the Americas, Saudi Arabia has a steep hierarchy which leads to a very structured line of bosses and leaders. The company should be a well-oiled machine by having early deadlines and managerial co-operation to help ease the stress of managers higher up the hierarchy. This is supported by a survey respondent stating that *"all of the companies I worked with used to apply the international standards which it force all leaders to work professionally"* (CCBS Survey, 2018). Due to this steep hierarchy, ranking up through the company leads to a large number of additional benefits that can include cars, houses and other luxury goods. It is common practice for parking places to be reserved for the elite members of the company which acts as both a reminder and an inspiration to others. This leads to employees staying in a single company due to commitment and loyalty as moving companies will make you less likely to get promotions. Due to this, Saudi Arabia is focused on the future rather than the present or past. As Saudi Arabia also has a strong uncertainty avoidance, companies will plan minute details to help achieve a smooth-running future. While other Arabic states (mainly Dubai) are trading culture and history for Western values and tourism, Saudi Arabia has begun to conserve their history and traditions. Saudi nationals are more likely to employ others for lower status jobs or manual labour so that they can keep their status in society as Saudis have *"negative social and cultural perceptions and attitudes towards manual and low status jobs"* (Achoui, 2009, p. 37). Saudization is the term used for the Saudi government's policy to force private sector firms to employ Saudis. In addition to the challenge of curbing unemployment, the government has also come under international pressure to reform its labour laws to ensure the better social protection of workers (Mellahi, 2007).

Saudi Arabia scores incredibly high on Hofstede's Power Distance dimension, meaning that hierarchical order is accepted and common. *"Hierarchy in an organization is seen as reflecting inherent inequalities, centralization is popular, subordinates expect to be told what to do and the ideal boss is a benevolent autocrat"* (Hofstede Insights, n.d). Traditionally, men are seen as being leaders, as women have limited opportunities to engage in strategic decision-making within a company. This is mainly due to the centralised decision-making within Saudi business and the limited power granted to Saudi women leaders (Alsubaie & Jones, 2017).

How Saudis achieve leadership empathy

Empathy is a necessity for a Saudi Arabian leader. As Khan notes, *"IQ intelligence is good, but Emotional intelligence is important for leadership"* (Khan, 28 March 2018). Researchers from Michigan State University state that Saudi Arabia is second in Empathy Rankings in the world (Chopik, O'Brien & Konrath, 2016). This could be due to the fact that *"Empathy is part of Saudi Arabian culture"* (Khan, 28 March 2018). Saudi Arabian families are dynastic in nature, allowing multiple generations to assume parental positions. This allows offspring to see faithful employees more empathetically, especially if they have worked for past generations. As a continuation of dynastic proof, families are more likely to employ other family members. However, this is not always optimal as family involvement in management negatively affects performance due to the general lack of professional competencies in families (Fouad, 2013). Despite its possible negative impact on the business, family connections remain a characteristic part of Saudi businesses: *"The right family connections is playing a role sometimes during selection and hiring and could be a power in governmental sectors more than the private. It is a culture actually"* (CCBS Survey, 2018). This is a double-edged sword as it is very difficult to penetrate the market if one is from another family. Historical prejudices still run true as tribal tensions are still prominent in modern day society.

Slovenia

Huib de Jong, Floris Valk & Danni Wang

Slovenia, the hidden gem in Central Europe, is spoilt with nature in many ways. It holds beautiful mountains, is water-abundant and almost 60% of it is covered with forests. It is situated near the Adriatic Sea between Italy and Croatia. The country in its current form split from Yugoslavia in the early nineties and is a parliamentary republic in Central Europe with parliament seated in its capital Ljubljana. The formerly communist country joined the Eurozone and the OECD last decade. Slovenia, with just over two million inhabitants, is a rather small country compared to their neighbours: Italy, Austria, Croatia and Hungary. Their extrovert Italian and Croatian neighbours consider the Slovenes introverted. The patriotic hearts of the Slovenes are honest, industrious, peaceable and family-oriented, but are ambitious in business and are among the wealthiest in Central Europe. The Slovenes have a short history as a sovereign country. Nonetheless, Slovenian leadership transitioned from a hierarchical culture to an egalitarian leadership style.

How the Slovenes characterise leaders

In the first place, we learn from Dimovski, Grah, Penger and Peterlin (2010) the definition of leadership in Slovenia: *"Authentic leaders point the followers into the right direction, gain their compliance for the mission of the organization and then motivate them to achieve the goals set together by the followers and leaders but furthermore they develop new leaders"* (Dimovski et al., 2010, p. 217). Whereas Dimvoski et al. (2010) focus on authentic leadership, Kovacic and Rus (2014, p. 16) compare competencies of Slovenian local leaders in healthcare with professional management. They suggest the gained position motivates leaders in healthcare as the next step in their medical career rather than a move away from the medical position into professional management. Not being in their natural habitat, healthcare leaders tend to lag behind on the higher standards of professional management. Professional leaders in Slovenia should be able to balance decision-making skills with relational and informational competencies to be viewed as a strong manager. Leaders are not too concerned with keeping current with their field of expertise. Compared to healthcare managers, who grew in their leadership role, commercial leaders are less disciplined and less efficient in their use of time (Kovacic & Rus, 2014).

Although culture does not change quickly, it is valuable to understand the future preferences. Pucko and Cater (2011), who use the GLOBE dimensions to define the cultural preferences towards leadership, focus on future managers in their research. They have discovered a preference for team-oriented and value-based leadership styles among Slovene leaders. A certain harmonisation of these leadership styles can be expected in the near future in Slovenia. Pucko and Cater (2011) conclude that managers should be effective in negotiations and well-informed in their management.

Local leadership analysis

In-country literature review

Some respected work on authentic leadership has been performed by the Faculty of Economics of the University of Ljubljana, under the professorship of Vlado Dimovski, economist and former Minister of Labour, Family and Social Affairs. His publications (with co-authors) are mainly connected to authentic leadership in learning organisations and conclude that *"the learning organization leverages the authentic leadership, which in return leverages the learning organization"* (Dimovski et al., 2010, p. 221). Continuous improvement in leadership within a country requires effort. Kvas and Seljak (2014) acknowledges this effort by measuring an increase in self-assessments of personal characteristics, like self-esteem, amongst nurse leaders over the past decade: nurses tend to identify themselves as intelligent, creative and interested in social issues.

A totally different approach to leadership can be observed by the research of Pfajfar, Uhan, Fang and Redek (2016), who compare business cultures of Slovenia with China based on proverbs. They conclude that a balance between individualistic and collectivistic leadership styles, *"each in the right measure, at the right time, pays off in performance"* (Pfajfar et al., 2016, p. 452).

A publication by Pucko and Cater (2011) slightly deviates from current leadership, focusing on perceptions of leadership by future managers. Future Slovenian leaders appreciate self-protective and autonomous leadership styles, as opposed to the charismatic, value-based and participative leadership styles valued by future leaders from the Czech Republic, Germany, Romania and Slovakia.

In-country leadership bestseller

One of the best-selling books about leadership in Slovenia is *Postani najboljši vodja* (Becoming the Best Leader), written by Marjan Račnik (2010). Račnik is a neurolinguistic programming coach (NLP) and an entrepreneur running various types of training and training workshops. Specialised in communications, public speaking, teamwork and especially leadership training, he covers not only leadership but also topics concerning life and work in general in the book. *Postani najboljši vodja* describes common pitfalls made by leaders, offers insights and instructions for changing from a classical manager to an authentic leader, as described earlier by Dimovski et al. (2010). The book is considered a useful guide for current and upcoming leaders, with its main focus on the development of managerial skills: how to become an accepted and respected leader (vodja, n.d.).

Local leadership book	
Title	Postani najboljši vodja
Author	Marjan Račnik
Publisher	Narodna in univerzitetna knjižnica, Ljubljana
Year	2010
ISBN	978-961-245-942-0

Understanding hierarchy in Slovenia

Prevodnik and Biloslavo (2009) conclude in their study that *"in Slovenia chief executives are more manager- than leader-oriented"* (p. 92). They also note *"that there is a kind of balance between manager-oriented chief executives and leader-oriented middle managers"* (Prevodnik & Biloslavo, 2009, p. 92). This tells us that from a CEO-perspective, being a leader is not the most important skill but being a good manager is. The middle management of Slovene companies nevertheless shows their leader-orientation. This statement indicates that employees traditionally looked at CEOs to be good at managing the company, but that middle management would be the real leaders of the employees within the hierarchy of Slovene companies.

The study also states that times are changing for Slovene leaders, due to the changing business environment. According to Prevodnik and Biloslavo (2009), the current leadership style is based on the transition that Slovene companies went through when these companies changed from the old self-governing mentality. During this transition, leaders were chosen based on their ability to lower cost through their entire supply chain and to focus the employees' attention on increasing capital. This transition in leadership style also has a direct impact on the hierarchy. In their study, Prevodnik and Biloslavo (2009) state that due to the changing business environment, leaders can perform well and give their best results. Nevertheless, they indicate that not all managers should disappear. They recommend leaders to take the place of managers for a while and the other way around (Prevodnik & Biloslavo, 2009).

Another aspect of hierarchy is the trust of employees in their leaders. In their studies, Andersen and Kovac (2013) state that trust is very important to Slovene employees and their managers. When looking at the data Hofstede (n.d.) gathered, you can see that a low masculinity score indicates that Slovenes expect their leaders to be caring for their employees. If leaders are not trusted, this level of care cannot be reached.

How Slovenes achieve leadership empathy

Although the business structure follows a top-down approach for business decisions, it is important to create empathy towards business choices, and it will be even more important in the future, according to Pucko and Cater (2011). Leaders in Slovenia are similar to hierarchical countries where respect towards authority is important, such as Germany and Austria. A leader is respected based on his or her personal knowledge and abilities.

Since status is considered important, it is impolite to speak ill of the business partners or their competitors. Focus on the qualities another brings to the table and decide if the business is one with a right of existence.

Clothing is important to be taken seriously in Slovenian business. Dress in conservative business attire, and dress with style. Companies usually have a business dress code, ranging from formal with the larger companies to business-casual with the smaller companies (Businessculture, n.d.).

To conclude, leaders in Slovenia achieve empathy by being a leader who decides in a group-oriented matter but takes the decision nonetheless. A leader is valued for his or her expertise and personal abilities. This is supported by Andersen and Kovac (2013): in Slovenia, *"managers (leaders) enjoy different degrees of trust from their subordinates"* (p. 303). Furthermore, Andersen and Kovac (2013) explain that the manager must *"show in action that he or she trusts his or her subordinates, promotes the interests of the subordinates, demonstrates an appreciation of his or her subordinates, and solves problems in an adequate way"* (p. 308). Naturally, it is more difficult for managers to gain the trust of the more remote subordinates than of those who are closer.

Spain

Jill Hoost, Niek Jacobsen & Kilian Schrijvers

Spain (*España*) is one of the biggest European countries, with a large percentage of its citizens living in Madrid, the capital of Spain (Instituto Nacional de Estadística, 2017). The main language in Spain is the Castilian form of Spanish. Other co-official languages are Basque, Catalan and Galician. The majority of Spaniards are Roman Catholic. The regional distinctions within the country are based on language and history, and the territorial ties remain strong, although the regional cultures were unified in the fifteenth century. The major regional cultures are Andalusian, Basque, Castilian, Catalan, Galician and Leonese.

The rich Spanish culture and enjoyable climate result in the country being one of the most popular tourist destinations in Europe (Eurostat, 2017). Spain's tourism industry has grown into the second-largest in the world, during the last four decades. According to a 2015 survey by the World Economic Forum, the country's tourism industry is among some of the most competitive the world. Besides tourism, the Spanish economy thrives on automotive, energy and agribusiness production (Instituto Nacional de Estadística, 2017).

According to Tomalin and Nicks (2012), Spain has three major business cultures: Madrid, Barcelona and Andalusia. However, between northern Spain, central Spain and the Basque Country, there are also significant differences. As stated by Dolan et al. (2004), the Spanish value efficacy, power, prestige and the co-existence of collective values in relation to work. Examples of collective values are a pleasant work atmosphere and strong teamwork. However, it has been noted that the Spanish population operates more within an individualist cultural context. Bearing those aspects in mind, this chapter will dive into a detailed analysis of the Spanish leadership style.

How the Spaniards characterise leaders

The Catholic tradition does not advocate the idea of individual leadership, but of collegiate authorities (Prieto, 1989). Standout individual acts are common but not applicable to leadership behaviour, which has a hierarchic aspect to it: the person at the top should lead a community when the situation calls for it.

According to Tomalin and Nicks (2012), the management structure in Spain is generally top-down, meaning that the boss holds the most power. All major decisions must be referred to or authorized by him or her and all discussions and management decisions will be taken at the top. As a result, a significant first meeting will be with the company chief, although employees may work operationally with a middle manager at their level with a responsibility level equal to theirs. In the event that the boss of a top-down managed company is absent, no decisions will be taken, and while lower management can champion proposals they do not have the authority to make the deciding call (Tomalin & Nicks, 2012).

This is in line with Spanish leaders being characterised as autocratic and charismatic, as reported by Lewis (2016). However, they work more from intuition than logic and are proud of their personal influence on all their staff members. Often possessing great human force, they are able to persuade and inspire people among all organisational levels and often see their decisions as final and irreversible.

Steven Guest (8 March 2018), a professor of Negotiation and Communication in Spain, states that he can see that most Spanish leadership styles (both managerial and political) are more transactional than transformational. He explains that *"[t]his has its roots in the culture and relatively recent development of the economy, into a knowledge and services-based model. Nevertheless, thanks to the variety of top-class business schools in Spain, there is a professionalisation of management that tops most developed countries"* (Guest, 4 March 2018).

Additionally, Gielen (4 April 2018), a Dutch credit and compliance analyst who has been active in Barcelona for many years, tells that hard work and staying in your role as a manager is a must have for any good Spanish leader. When one is working hard and helping co-workers with their questions, he or she is seen as a triumphant leader in the eyes of his co-workers. As stated by Gielen: *"It is a win-win relationship"* (4 April 2018). He also describes good leadership in Spain as respectful, hardworking and helpful. He believes that the most difficult aspect for a leader in Spain is the presence of nepotism is. Therefore, he concludes that it is easier to get a job if you have a wide network of family and friends (Gielen, 4 April 2018).

Survey results and what local respondents say

The CCBS Survey (2018) on Spanish leadership gathered over twenty-five responses from local and experienced leadership professionals. While the results show clear differences of opinion on leadership aspects, there are also similar views on leadership and leadership styles within Spain that can aid in forming a general impression of Spanish leadership.

First of all, opinions are divided when it comes to changing a management decision that has already been made. A marginal majority of the respondents feel like it cannot be changed easily. There are also different qualities that are expected of a good leader. According to the participants, employees look up to a professional when he or she is a powerful decision-maker, is a good listener, has organisational experience, has access to the right networks and is resourceful.

Secondly, there are also similarities in the leadership style appreciated by respondents. CCBS findings reveal that managers have to spend time on the personal well-being of their staff. Also, most respondents disagree with having to keep a level of personal distance as a leader, in order to maintain the right level of respect (CCBS Survey, 2018). This means that Spanish leaders attach more value to the relationship with their employees than to prestige. This results in a more relationship-oriented leadership style.

Also, most professionals agree that if necessary, a manager might confront team members or subordinates during a staff meeting, to obtain targeted results. They prefer hearing criticism in a direct manner, during a staff meeting. Additionally, missing a deadline is more or less seen as a failure. According to the respondents, a manager should also encourage some competition within a team, in order to achieve better results in the long-run.

Furthermore, the majority of the respondents note that within their organisation, rules cannot be bent by the employees. As one respondent puts it: *"Rules can be challenged, but red lines can't be crossed"* (CCBS Survey, 2018). Besides, in Spanish organisations, the procedures will be followed up by the employees. Only a few professionals achieve independence with regards to following the rules. This means that value is attached to the rules and procedures in the Spanish business culture. Interestingly, most of the respondents disagree with the statement that an academic title on a business card or in an e-mail is important. The same applies to addressing leaders by their title. Nearly all the respondents admit to hardly ever doing so. The large majority agrees that they can address their leader by his or her first name (CCBS Survey, 2018). According to the respondents, the following titles can be used when addressing leaders:

When talking about equality of the sexes, most of the participants are neutral about the statement that men and women should have equal access to senior leadership positions. However, there is a clear difference between the leadership styles of men and women in Spain. One respondent says: *"Women are more intuitive and show less confidence"* (CCBS Survey, 2018).

Lastly, the respondents think that the most suitable time to schedule a business meeting is between 09:00 and 11:00 in the morning. Other typical characteristics of the Spanish leadership culture include less formality, flat hierarchy, openness and teamwork. One respondent also points out a few key aspects of Spanish leadership: *"Natural leaders are able to get the most of the contributors. The big issue comes from the culture, the job, and that team leaders can be changed easily. There are no hard commitments, resulting in a conflict with one's personal life. Very similar to millennials loyalty"* (CCBS Survey, 2018).

Local leadership analysis

In-country literature review

Multiple Spanish studies on leadership reveal an authentic leadership style to be most effective. A study by Valsania et al. (2012) has shown that the influence of the authentic leadership style is stronger when behaviours are impersonal and directed towards the company, rather than towards individuals. These findings agree with those from previous research on the subject (Moriano et al., 2011). It shows that authentic leadership can positively affect the worker's behaviour. Additionally, there are numerous studies linking leadership to organisational processes. Native authors have attributed successful leadership to increased performance through organisational learning and innovation. Aragón-Correa, García-Morales and Cordón-Pozo (2007) conclude in a recent research that leadership has a strong significant influence on organisational learning in Spain. Since learning directly influences innovation and innovation positively affects performance, leadership therefore contributes to greater performance within Spanish firms. Other authors studied the efficacy of leadership training programmes.

A recent study by Quesada, Pineda-Herrero and Espona (2011) shows that emotional intelligence training of leaders is a key aspect to the success of companies, but the efficacy of these programmes is in the process of development. Whenever senior and middle managers fail to show an interest in their followers, trainees are hindered in applying their newly acquired emotional intelligence skills to their workplace.

Dr Ruben Llop: a Spanish leadership scholar

In order to get a good perspective on Spanish leadership, multiple videos of Spanish leadership scholars have been studied. Dr Ruben Llop is a Spanish leadership scholar and the founder of an institute for transformational leadership. Llop (2016) states that leaders must be competent enough to motivate and inspire their employees in such a way that they become more committed. Llop adds that as a leader, one is not able to give employees all the required commitment: the employees have to do their best and think on their own. According to him, commitment is the best way to improve operations and achieve the intended results. He also emphasises that even if a company has hundreds of key performance indicators, commitment is key in showing how efficient the strategic direction is. He believes that *"In order to make any transformation within an organisation, there is only one thing that must change: the individual's willingness to commit themselves to get this new future"* (Llop, 2016). Additionally, Llop argues that leadership is when leaders enable their employees to decide on their own and are committed to delivering the best work they can. It is at this point, he notes, where transformation begins and where a leader must realise if he or she is able to persuade others in an honest and inspiring way. As a leader, you should be able to answer the question in which directions employees want to go and how they want to achieve their goals. Llop concludes that knowing that answer will improve the process of achieving the intended results and of getting treated the way you deserve, which is professionally, in an honest way, with direct and clear communication. Also, he admits that *"At the end of the day, leadership is being able to imagine a better future of an organisation and how to make it happen"* (Llop, 2016). Hereby, he concludes that leaders have to build on the relational aspect with their teams, to build momentum and passion.

Rudmer Bosga: a cross-cultural professional

Rudmer Bosga, a partner business manager at SAP Business Solutions, was also interviewed on his views on leadership. He provided interesting insights into the Spanish business culture, thanks to his experience in working with different cultures at SAP Barcelona. Bosga (17 April 2018) talks about the inherent culture of Spain, where family plays an important role. In Spain, it is seen as normal that family still makes decisions for their kids, even when they are 30-40 years old. It is a very warm culture, according to him, although there is a negative side to it, as people tend to be absorbed by their family situation. Spaniards also tend to be both individualistic and collectivistic, since they always think with their family in mind. He also states that pure Spanish companies tend to have leaders who have the Spanish culture embedded in their leadership style. His own experience in smaller, Spanish-dominated companies dates back 30 years ago. Back then, Spanish managers worked with authority and strong character. They also imposed fear in others, in order to get things done. Bosga believes that the Spanish leadership style has changed and is becoming more and more modern and international. Especially in Barcelona, where the work-environment is internationally focused and cultures range from Spanish to Belgic and American. Additionally, he illustrates the difference in leadership between the northern and southern parts of Spain: *"I think it's more about that the more south you go, the more stronger characters you see, and the more north, the more realistic or down to earth the leaders are"* (Bosga, 17 April 2018). As stated by Bosga, it is important to understand what drives your people as a manager. Hereby, he emphasises that employees want to be valued by their company. This means that value-giving is an important aspect to consider as a leader in Spain. Moreover, he believes that a good leader makes his followers go a long way for the company. You have to know the worth of your people's time and understand that they have private lives as well. *"If you're a manager, what drives you is making a successful team and making people grow"* (Bosga, 17 April 2018).

In-country leadership bestseller

In 2018, Margarito Mayo published her business bestseller about leadership and how leaders become and remain authentic. She is an award-winning researcher and professor of leadership and organisational behaviour at IE Business School in Madrid and is originally from Spain (Mayo, 2018).

According to Mayo, a confidence crisis lies at the heart of Spanish contemporary corporate leadership. *"Since the financial crisis, distrust of employers among the workforce has dramatically increased, due to a lack of authentic leadership"* (Mayo, 2018). Entitled, *Yours Truly,* the book is based on inspirational examples from a lot of different leaders, as well as more than two decades of research, examining missing link in research into authentic leadership: how leaders strive for success, excellence and constant renewal, whilst remaining true to themselves. She introduces three pillars, on which success rests: Heart, Habits and Harmony. These characteristics differentiate authentic from non-authentic leaders. The book provides a measurable guide, presented in a practical framework to develop your authentic power as a leader. It consists of three components: the contagious passion that wins the hearts of others, setting new habits of learning to empower people and enhancing harmony by building authentic contexts. It is a timely, global, research-based and very practical book.

Local leadership book	
Title	Yours Truly
Author	Staying Authentic in Leadership and Life
Author	Margarita Mayo
Publisher	Bloomsbury Publishing
Year	2018
ISBN	9781472950918

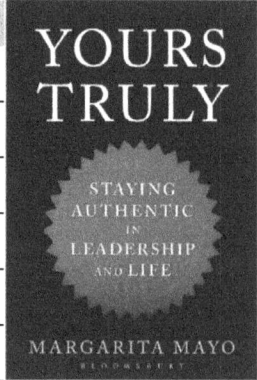

YOURS TRULY

STAYING AUTHENTIC IN LEADERSHIP AND LIFE

MARGARITA MAYO
BLOOMSBURY

"Yours Truly captures the value of authentic leadership in transforming organizations, stripping away the seemingly magical, innate charismatic qualities of leaders in order to showcase a less mysterious and more practical process that can be followed by anyone" (Mayo, 2018).

Spanish leadership YouTube review

Next to Spanish literature sources, YouTube videos have revealed a lot of relevant information on leadership. This chapter will give an overview of what a local expert has to say on the topic, from a Spanish perspective. Margarita Mayo, the author of *Yours Truly* is also present in other media channels. In a video interview, she compares leadership with the dance, tango. She explains that tango is all about improvisation. Since the business world nowadays has become very fast, leaders must be able to think on their feet. According to her, leaders should innovate and create their unique choreography, to be able to adapt to the fast business world and the ever-changing environment. *"It takes two to tango, one who leads and one who follows. Typically, in tango the man is the leader, and the woman is the follower. But in modern versions of tango, those leading and following negotiate their roles on the dance floor. Just like in organisations"* (Mayo, 2013).

Thereby, she means that roles depend on who has more expertise on the matter. Tango is a social activity, just like doing business. Mayo notes that dancing with someone is a way to meet new people establishing a fast connection. However, she also explicitly notes that it is very important for people to respect the space and rhythm of others, just like in leadership. *"Leaders provide a vision, but that needs to fit with the strategy of the whole organization. At the end, leadership is about passion and compassion: sharing what you like with others on the dance floor"* (Mayo, 2013).

Understanding hierarchy in Spain

According to several studies done across Europe, Spanish leaders show the highest need of hierarchy within an organisation. This is supported by O'Connell and Prieto (1998), whose research reveals that Spain has a rather high score for power distance. Thus, a hierarchical distance is accepted and little justification for unequal power distribution is needed. Hierarchy is evident in most Spanish businesses and even small family firms. The government-controlled sector shows more traditional characteristics, which include a large amount of respect for superiors (Kooyers, 2015). The Spanish language also reflects this eagerness to show respect, as it has a form of conjugation *'usted'* that is particularly used for speaking to authority figures (Chhokar, Brodbeck & House, 2008).

The ideal boss is charitable yet autocratic, making most of the decisions while keeping the best interest of the employees in mind (Hofstede, 2010). According to Gielen (4 April 2018), there is a big distance between a leader and employees on the work floor, but not in private life.

Back (2012) argues that in Spanish businesses, it may be more prevalent for the boss to work independently from employees. They dress, act and speak in a way that differentiates them from subordinate workers. On the other hand, as the new generation takes over family businesses, they are more influenced by the American business style, where young leaders use more participative methods.

How the Spaniards achieve leadership empathy

A study done by Mittal and Dorfman (2012) shows that the endorsement of empathy in Latin Europe is low. Latin Europe, which Spain is part of, has the lowest score out of all researched countries. Spaniards place a greater emphasis on reason and intellect than emotional values which has contributed to the lower endorsement of empathy.

As stated by Gielen (4 April 2018), Spanish workers look up to the managers and directors, in contrast with other cultures, such as the Dutch, but adds that Spanish empathy can change by the day or even hour. The reason behind this ever-changing empathy is the fact that Spanish people take good care of themselves. If a Spanish leader is to show empathy, he or she must talk openly, be agreeable and show interest during conversations, according to Gielen. However, when there are more people involved in the conversation, they tend to act on behalf of an authority.

Lastly, Gielen (4 April 2018) thinks that the most important aspect of the relationship between a Spanish leader and his or her followers is the expectation of hard work. Also, the Spanish leader's inability to take criticism well can also be problematic. The research from Mittal and Dorfman (2012) shows that employees in Spain do not receive a lot of empathy from their leader, but when the conversation is not about work, everybody is very friendly and approachable.

Switzerland

Marelle Schimmel, Bart de Mooij & Arjan Möller

Switzerland is better known as *Confœderatio Helvetica* (CH) and is famous for its neutral placement during historical conflicts between multiple countries. Besides as a neutral state, Switzerland is also known for its jewellery, clockworks, chocolate, cheese, mountains, all-season tourism and its highly trusted financial market. The country is located in Central Europe and has borders with Germany, France, Italy, Liechtenstein and Austria. A remarkable fact is that most Swiss speak multiple languages, including German, French and Italian. The majority of the Swiss population speaks German. Switzerland is not a member of the European Union; therefore, the Swiss Franc (CHF) is the national currency instead of the most commonly used currency - the Euro. Switzerland's economy is highly dependent on foreign trade. In 2016, the total exports in 2016 amounted to CHF 302 billion, and the overall imports, on their part, amounted to CHF 268 billion. The service sectors - banks, insurance, and tourism – make up a significant share of Switzerland's foreign trade (OEC, n.d.).

How the Swiss characterise leaders

Swiss leaders are known to be result-orientated. In addition to achieving results, an ideal Swiss leader is said to be a people's person, efficacious and innovative. The Swiss know that they have to innovate to keep ahead of the competition. As a CEO from Basel points out, to achieve success as a leader, it is wise to be pragmatic and show respect to one's co-workers (CCBS Survey, 2018). Dietmar Treichel (27 March 2018) concurs that typical Swiss Leadership is predominantly focused on community, competition and innovation. Therefore, these three aspects can be regarded as the key performance indicators of what might be expected of a Swiss Leader. Treichel explained in an interview, that the cultural background forms this behaviour. For instance, he explains the tendency towards competitiveness as a result of the fact that *"Switzerland is an island in Europe and has to be strong to compete with the other European countries"* (27 March 2018). How leaders use these behavioural indicators depends on the type of corporate culture and type of branch. In the Cross-Cultural Business Skills Survey of 2017, a Swiss manager said: *"Leadership in Switzerland is somewhat like the nature of the country itself. Switzerland is a complex melting pot of cultures - the Italian, French and German inhabitants of Switzerland, plus a major contingent of expat managers employed by global companies. As a result, there is not a 'standard' leadership or management style in this country that is consistent across the regions and cultures".* Although it is not simple to characterise a typical Swiss leader, one can deduce, based on the results of the CCBS Survey (2018), a Swiss leader ought to be humble, not be speaking out loud, be pragmatic, not dogmatic and show an ability to socialise with the co-workers on a professional level. Avolio and Gardner (2005) support this view that Swiss leaders are expected to be pragmatic and efficiency-oriented. They also point out that Swiss employees will only accept a leader if he or she illustrates high ability for consent and modest manners (Avolio & Gardner, 2005).

Survey results and what local respondents say

Around fifty Swiss local and experienced professionals have responded to the questions of the Cross-Cultural Business Skills Survey (2018). Various leaders from different branches and backgrounds were asked to give their opinion about leadership in Switzerland. The most important results of this survey can be summarised as follows: when we take a look at the outcome we can see that 85% of the employees can address their leader in Switzerland by their first name (CCBS Survey, 2018). This has also been confirmed by Dietmar Treichel (27 March 2018), director of the Institute of Communication and Leadership in Luzern. This gives perspective on the relationship between leaders and employees.
It is therefore not surprising that a majority of the respondents indicate that a manager must actively spend time on the personal welfare of the team members, as confirmed by Gion-Pieder Pfister, CEO of Swissport in Basel (CCBS Survey, 2018; Pfister, 13 April 2018). Most of the respondents have a Swiss nationality. However, there are significant differences between regions in Switzerland. An education programme director explains: *"Switzerland is not a homogeneous country in terms of leadership. There are three different regions: western part is French (but not exactly as the French), the southern part is Italian (but not exactly as the Italians), and the north-eastern part is German (but not exactly as the Germans). This makes the whole issue quite difficult. As the labour market is requesting the employees and especially leaders to be flexible, they become used to different leadership styles and later on adapt their own style"* (CCBS Survey, 2017). According to Dietmar Treichel: *"There is no typical Swiss leader"* (27 March 2018). Secondly, the Swiss professionals consider that

employees look up to a leader on the basis of organisational experiences. Some professionals explain in an extra comment that: *"empathy is also an important leadership experience"* (CCBS Survey, 2018). Finally, there is a frequent input about Swiss result-oriented leadership. According to a Swiss CFO, specific to Swiss leadership are *"the respectful relations between management and lower levels and the performance-driven cultures"* another professional explains that typical to it is *"[its] pragmatism and emphasis of results"* (CCBS Survey, 2018).

Local leadership analysis

In-country literature review

Werner R. Mueller and Jens O. Meissner (2005), professors at the University of Basel, researched in their article, – "What is the Meaning of Leadership. A Guided Tour through a Swiss-German Leadership Landscape", what leadership means in Switzerland. The research group is Swiss leaders from the German-speaking part. The research results are based on the following five leadership functions: position, binding commitment, relationship to the business, social proximity and authenticity. The first function concerns 'the position' of managers. Respondents complain about managers who cannot decide, who hide behind experts and who avoid conflicts. They need a leader with knowhow and one who does not hesitate to make a decision. The second function is 'binding commitment.' It suggests being relevant as a leader requires one to not be ambiguous about one's position, but also to consistently put the decisions that have been made into practice and should reflect himself or herself as a leader. A leader should have self-commitment ('walk your talk'). The third function is the 'relation to the business'. A leader needs a number of attention points in relation to his business. He or she must show and generate dedication and stand by his or her decision. This must reveal the relationship between a leader and the company. The fourth function is 'social proximity', most interviewed managers agree with the following statement from a CEO of a globally operating company: *"Every leader, of course, wants to be loved. I think that is normal. You want that the others like you and consider you are a good boss"* (CCBS Survey, 2018). About the fifth function 'authenticity' they describe that leaders can follow, read and learn how to behave as a perfect leader but stay true to yourself. These five functions together illustrate a prominent topic and show leadership dilemmas in the German-speaking part of Switzerland (Mueller & Meissner, 2015).

Gion-Pieder Pfister: CEO of Swissport

A vice-president and CEO of Swissport from Basel was interviewed, and he gave his point of view as a leader. Gion-Pieder Pfister has a lot of experience as a leader in the aviation branch. He was a general manager and CEO for companies like Swiss International Air Lines and EVP Cargo. As Pfister (13 April 2018) explains, Switzerland is by nature a land of comprise and respect. These aspects reflect in the Swiss way of leadership. Leaders are not controversial or democratic but more consensus-oriented. As a Swiss leader, you should talk to the staff about their opinions, to keep them satisfied and to make them a part of the company or team. In Switzerland, a leader has a collaborative relationship with his or her staff. In this relationship, it is clear what a company expects of the performance of the co-workers. Therefore, the Swiss are also result-oriented. The markets where Swiss companies operate are very competitive, that is why their leaders are steering on high performance. Besides high performance, it is a must to have a very effective process to stay ahead of the competition. The Swiss companies expect that leaders are very innovative and pragmatic. About hierarchy, Pfister says that leaders will create a consensus with their staff, but at the end of the day it is up to the leader to make a decision. He adds that the relationship between a leader and a co-worker is based on respect. Leaders should treat co-workers as human, but both know that they have a professional understanding of what a leader and a co-worker can expect from each other. Pfister (13 April 2018) claims that this is his way of empathising with his staff is a humanistic approach based on mutual respect.

Prof Dr Dietmar Treichel MAS MBA: Swiss scholar and trainer

Dietmar Treichel is a native scholar in leadership and cross-cultural trainer who has a MAS and an MBA and is a director at the Institute of Communication and Leadership in Luzern. He was interviewed for this book to offer us insights into the subjects: leadership, empathy and hierarchy in Switzerland. He points out that community, competition and innovation are the main ingredients of a Swiss Leader. Switzerland is an island between multiple countries. As he claims the Swiss feel the pressure to perform, therefore, to stay competitive, they have to be innovative to keep ahead of their opponents (Treichel, 27 March 2018). Typically, the Swiss will not be vocal about their opinions and achievements. In Switzerland it is not good to stand out. A leader should collaborate with his or her team to achieve goals. The Swiss are result-oriented; a Swiss leader is considered successful when he or she achieves results with the group as planned or achieves goals above what was planned. Hierarchy is more like a formal and structural setting for a company than a business culture that runs on authority and status. Hierarchy is functional and everybody in a company understands his or her position. For example, to the question: "Do executive boards have an 'open door' policy?" Treichel says that it depends on of what kind of branch the company is in. For instance, a production company will not likely have an 'open door' policy while a soft skills company, like a marketing agency, are more likely to have one. Furthermore, he notes that in Switzerland, it is not the Swiss culture that is important in a company, but the culture of the company itself is. To empathise with the co-workers a leader should know the background of his staff, so he or she knows how to empathise (Treichel, 27 March 2018).

In-country leadership bestseller

One of the best-selling books about leadership is *Leadership– Best Practices und Trends*, written by Prof Dr Heike Buch, Dr Stefan Krummaker and Dr Bernd Vogel in 2012. The book shows how you can activate the energy of companies for maximum performance, just as modern forms of leadership make use of successful companies, and how you can bring high dynamics into the work processes without falling into the trap of acceleration.

Local leadership book	
Title	Leadership
Author	Best practices und Trends
Author	Heike Buch, Stefan Krumaker and Bernd Vogel
Publisher	Springer Gabler
Year	2012
ISBN	978-3-8349-9120-1

Switzerland leadership YouTube review

On YouTube, The Schweizer Kader Organisation makes videos of Swiss leaders that they interview about their business and their idea of leadership in their company. The YouTube series is called: "Leadership, the Swiss way". The most interviewees explain that Swiss management is a collaboration between managers and the workers on the floor. As Henri Meier says *"in der Schweizer Gemeindeist des viel stärker usammenarbeitenZwischenManagement und Mittarbeiter"* The Schweizer Kader Organisation, 2018e). Another interviewee, Eva Jaisli, explains that a leader in Switzerland needs inspirational power, innovation, creativity and responsibility. The management and the workers need these indicators to make high-quality products and provide a good service. Bernhard Heusler points out that leadership must be in collaboration with the workers. For example, by looking together to problems and discussing the options for a solution. This approach makes the collaboration credible for the employees and makes them feel involved. Eventually, management makes the final decisions. Switzerland is a country with a high level of technology with a sustainable solution (The Schweizer Kader Organisation, 2018).

Understanding hierarchy in Switzerland

Switzerland does not have a general type of hierarchy. Marek Pietrzyk (2017) describes that the Swiss have multiple management hierarchies. The source of multiple hierarchy styles comes from the multi-culture society of Switzerland. This finding reinforces those by Hofstede Insights (n.d.). The following characterises the German-Swiss style: being independent, hierarchy for convenience only, equal rights, superiors accessible, coaching leader, management facilitates and empowers. On this dimension, there is a vast difference with the French-speaking part of Switzerland, where people accept a hierarchical order in which everybody has a place and which needs no further justification. That means the French part has a clear hierarchical structure where every employee has his own place and responsibilities. However, nearly two-thirds of Switzerland consists of a German-speaking area. Because of this, the focus in this paragraph is in the German-speaking region (Chhokar, Brodbeck & House, 2013). Frauendorfer, Schmidt Mast, Sanchez-Cortes and Gatica-Perez (2015) found in a case study, presented in the article "Emergent Power Hierarchies and Group Performance", that a Swiss group that is led by a manager with a greater power distance style will deliver what is asked, but the manager with a more flattened hierarchy and a more emergent approach will create a more constructive work atmosphere. In Switzerland, there is a close link between the leader and the employee. Swiss leaders have a function as role models. According to Müller (1990), the authority of a leader will be accepted by his co-workers as he or she shows honourable and competent behaviour. Bergmann (1990) confirms that Swiss leaders have to work as long and as hard as their employees; they are not supposed to see themselves as more valuable than others because of their position. Swiss leaders do not make a distinction based on their rank, function, age or sex (Chhokar, Brodbeck & House, 2013). This is consistent with the results of the dimensions of Hofstede. On Hofstede's Power Distance scale, Switzerland scores a low 34 out of 100, which shows that Switzerland communication is direct and participative (Hofstede Insights, n.d.) Gion-Pieder Pfister (13 April 2018) agrees that leaders have to listen to their co-workers to get consensus before taking a decision. Although, he points out that at the end of the day a leader has to make a decision alone. Dietmar Treichel (27 March 2018) confirms that a Swiss leader is always looking for consensus, but only the leader can make the decision. According to Andre Valente, a Swiss CEO in the financial sector, Swiss leaders tend to understate and not over-expose their position (CCBS Survey, 2017). As an executive director from the banking sector points out in our survey (CCBS Survey, 2017), Swiss companies and leaders are very consensus-oriented but also hierarchical. About the level of decision making Cris Wilbur (CCBS Survey, 2017), a chief HR officer, notes that decision-making should happen at the right level in an organisation. There are always circumstances that require flexibility.

How the Swiss achieve leadership empathy

From the results of the CCBS Survey (2018), we can conclude that empathy is important in Switzerland. The research has shown that more than 75% of the respondents tend to care about their employees (CCBS Survey, 2018). Another fact is that the Swiss tend to look for solidity and reliability in the people they have to work with. This is why it is important to be in control of your emotions, private life and financial arrangement (Chhokar, Brodbeck & House, 2013). This is also confirmed by the article "The Essential Guide to Customs and Culture" (Culture Smart) which states that being respected is more important than being liked. Their style of communication also reflects this. According to Lewis (2006) property is much more important than affection, though when the Swiss begin to like you, they go out of their way to be friendly. In essence, they believe in mutual respect, which is built on trust as well as open and upfront communication (Lewis, 2006). Meetings are often by appointment. You should be clean, well-dressed, and it is important to be polite, even if you are bored out of your mind. Meanwhile, Dietmar Treichel (27 March 2018) notes, that the Swiss are humble in meetings and do not speak their opinions out loud. Gion-Pieder Pfister explains that Swiss staff have multiple job opportunities, and a Swiss leader will need to empathise to obtain respect and appreciation of the staff (13 April 2018).

Ukraine

Polina Burmistrova, Elize Wester & Anouk Verburg

In 1991, after the breakup of the Soviet Union, a new country appeared on the map of the world - Ukraine (Україна). The name refers to 'the land near the border' - U (near) and Krai (border). With an area of more than 600,000 square kilometres, Ukraine is the second largest country in Europe. The capital of Ukraine, Kiev, was founded in 482 AD, which is earlier than most cosmopolitan cities, such as Moscow, Tokyo, Berlin, New York or Los Angeles (Gazarian, 2015). Among other interesting facts, Kiev is the home to the deepest metro station in the world. Furthermore, the city claims to have the third busiest McDonald's in the world. Ukrainian nature is beautiful and diverse, with the Carpathian Mountains in the north and the Black Sea coast in the south. It is a lesser-known fact that Ukraine has the biggest desert in Europe, the size of which can be compared to Mauritius. Ukraine maintains close relationships with its European neighbours, particularly Poland (Savery, 2012). In terms of the world economy, Ukraine is seen as the breadbasket of Europe. Its large agricultural industry accounts for 25 percent of the global black soil, called *'chernozem'*. Currently, Ukraine has the fourth largest number of IT professionals in the world. Ukraine is a country full of contrasts. Having an understanding of its traditions and abundant culture is essential when doing business in Ukraine.

How Ukrainians characterise leaders

A common issue that has impacted on Ukrainian leadership over the past twenty years is the collapse of the USSR. Soviet influence still affects organisational management and hierarchy. According to the CCBS leadership survey (2018), having a strong charismatic personality is essential to any outstanding Ukrainian leader. Additionally, Gornostai states in the survey conducted for this book that: *"Our business leaders are often more flexible and more driven-by-pressure than in other countries, which is the result of the fast market growth/decline and hard doing business conditions (and investment climate) in the country"* (CCBS Survey, 2018). Meanwhile, most Ukrainian business organisations build the impression of living up to the old standards and idealising leaders. Employees with a lower status within the company tend to avoid disagreements. On the other hand, the young generation of Ukrainians has increasingly come under the influence of the Western way of doing business. They strive for equality with less idealisation of their leaders. The CEO of Arricano Real Estate, Mikhail Merkulov, states the following: *"As every human being, a leader should not always appear to be perfect. We all have an abnormality. Look for unusual! The only way you will find leaders who will lead your business to tomorrow's success"* (Pavlushenko, 2018). Ukrainian journalists discussed that 'business heroes' are breaking the stereotype of the Ukrainian leader, which is achieved by prioritising creativity, taking risks or being ambitious. The authors emphasise that the most valuable skills are the constant curiosity and the desire to take on more responsibility. For Roshupkina (2018) an enterprising leader will not just be able to manage others with genius but will have a more complete knowledge of his or her 'product' (Roshupkina, 2018). It can be concluded that the stereotypical Ukrainian leader is not as common as before. Nowadays, leaders tend to be more flexible and do business according to successful global practices.

Survey results and what local respondents say

Results from the CCBS Survey (2018) in Ukraine shows that there are some considerable differences in leadership styles. Some businesses lean towards conservative leadership, while others are very progressive. *"It is of big difference if the branch in Ukraine is representing an EU company or a purely Ukrainian one. I am managing an EU branch in Ukraine and I see a huge difference from other Ukrainian companies in regards to management"* (CCBS Survey, 2018).

A key concept in Ukrainian leadership is trust. As one of our survey respondents stated: *"Building trust within the team is most important"* (CCBS Survey, 2018). This shows that relationships are more personalised rather than task-oriented. Relationship-oriented leadership focuses on supporting, motivating and developing employees, all leading to building healthy relationships. For this type of leadership, communication is key. It is not surprising that more than half of the survey respondents agree that a manager should actively spend time on the personal well-being of the team members (CCBS Survey, 2018).

Furthermore, the survey shows that women and men do not have equal access to senior leadership positions. *"In Ukraine, women become leaders very rarely. Their role as wives and mothers of leaders can influence decisions"* (CCBS Survey, 2018). Even though women may have less access to power, their advice and opinion is still widely sought.

Moreover, one of our respondents states that: *"Women are normally more autocratic [than] democratic because otherwise it might be hard for them to achieve their goals"* (CCBS Survey, 2018). This quote implies that women in Ukraine have indeed a harder time becoming a leader than men. Due to the historical patterns of strong patriarchy in the country, citizens might find it difficult to accept a woman as their leader. *"If a woman becomes a leader, she has to have guts, otherwise she won't be a leader for long"* (CCBS Survey, 2018). Ukrainians are naturally very dominant. A popular proverb states that: "Among two men you will see three kings" (*"Два пани - три гетьмани"*). This illustrates the nature of the dominating archetype in the Ukrainian philosophy of leadership (CCBS Survey, 2018). Three-quarters of the survey respondents agree that employees may not bend the rules without asking. As one of our respondents puts it: *"Leaders don't encourage changes so much. It is better to follow the rules."* This can also be explained by the dominant position the leader would usually assume (CCBS Survey, 2018).

Lastly, a leader in Ukraine is expected to be a powerful decision maker (CCBS Survey, 2018). Final decisions are usually made by the one in charge. This is in contrast with other Western countries where employees from any position can take part in the decision-making process. A Ukrainian leader has to obtain and hold on to as much control as possible. He or she may make use of micromanagement, time tracking and strictness in meeting deadlines. Without proper control, they would face adversity (CCBS Survey, 2018).

Local leadership analysis

In-country literature review
The history of communism in Ukraine often builds the impression of extremely strong-opinionated executives. Slavic people describe them as the figures which have absolute control over subordinates, calculating every company move. According to the literature published up to ten years after the USSR has collapsed, the key difference between Ukrainian and Slavic leadership styles is the management culture and top organisational community. A variety of resources also highlights the public avoidance of such top management, who often maintained a fraternal order and sought increased effectiveness by interacting in smaller groups. Modern Ukrainian business schools use teaching materials that promote close and friendly relationships between the managers and subordinates. "[…] *ознакою сучасного лідера є прагнення не зосередити у своїх руках усю повноту влади, а наділяти нею підлеглих, […] й залучення*

всіх спів робітників до вирішення організаційних проблем. Відтак, лідери мають створювати середовище, сприятливе для співробітників і взаємної підтримки." (Драч, 2015). The above-mentioned quote of Irina Drach, Doctor of Pedagogical Sciences in the University of Management and Psychology, explains the main characteristics of the modern leader who disrupts the traditional cycle of top management. Such leaders create a favourable atmosphere between the working employees, which eventually leads to an effective and supportive workplace setup.

Svitlana Plotnytska: a Ukrainian leadership scholar
Svitlana Plotnystka, a professor of Management and Administration at Kharkiv University of Economy in Ukraine, provided local, academic knowledge on the topic of Ukrainian leadership. In an interview, Plotnytska identifies the origin of Ukrainian leadership and the most common leadership patterns that one should be aware of. Plotnytska correlates the leadership techniques used in Ukraine to the leadership philosophy of the United States: "*The development of the Ukrainian management model takes place under the influence of modern American schools [...].*" (Plotnytska, 21 March 2018). The US model of building an efficient workplace environment is used by Ukrainian universities as an example of the best leadership practices. To get a deeper understanding of Ukrainian leadership, Plotnytska explains that the modern Ukrainian management models can be divided into three different types. The first and most common model is the socialist (Soviet Union) one. "*This model is maintained solely by Ukrainian enterprises that are operating on the domestic market with traditional products*" (Plotnytska, 21 March 2018).

The second most common leadership pattern is very interesting and unusual. Plotnytska (21 March 2018) explains it as a matter of common sense. "*It is used in newer organisations, without any special managerial education. Respect for management is shown, but in practice people are guided by common sense*" (21 March 2018). In this case, business is ruled by leaders who base their decisions solely on intuition. An example is small-scale farm goods, presented on farmer's markets in the big cities. These small businesses are usually owned by one family. It does not involve business planning or decision-making for reaching long-term goals. The third type of management is employed by foreign joint ventures, which have decided to do business in Ukraine. Frequently, a more Westernised model of management is presented in such companies. "*[...] the staff of these enterprises undergoes special training in management; and claim to have the best European and American practices* (Plotnytska, 21 March 2018).
All in all, Ukrainian leadership is currently in the middle of a transition from the

matured USSR approach represented by the senior managers to the fast-paced Westernised business models of young Ukrainians. There is a tendency towards flat hierarchy and less directing, within the business structure.

Marta Sydoryak: a Ukrainian leadership trainer

Marta Sydoryak the programme coordinator at the Ukrainian Leadership Academy, was also asked to express her views on leadership: *"Other countries are becoming interested in working with Ukraine, since Ukraine has turned more towards the West, as opposed to their long-lasting relationship with Russia"* (Sydoryak, 16 March 2018). The Ukrainian business culture is more progressive than one might think. *"A typical Ukrainian leader would be young, primarily with some kind of Western education or experience"* (Sydoryak, 16 March 2018). Most leaders are progressive and lean towards a Western style of doing business. Having many young leaders is great on one hand because young people are active and full of energy and are usually open to new opportunities. On the other hand, young leaders usually lack experience (Sydoryak, 16 March 2018).

The relationship between a leader and the employees is usually informal and open. Ukraine is more a relationship-oriented than task-oriented culture. A lot of time is invested in networking and making acquaintances. The leader is not only a 'boss' but also somebody the employee can relate to and speak to, on the same level (Sydoryak, 16 March 2018). One might think that Ukraine would have quite a conservative business culture due to its history. However, this interview shows that Ukraine has made some rapid developments in the past years, which have created a modern business culture, full of young and well-educated professionals.

In-country leadership writing

The popular impact of American authors on Ukrainian leadership is increasingly noticeable. The native scientific journals and books about leadership in Ukraine often contain a large part of the concepts and theories of North American management models. Nevertheless, a Ukrainian doctor of Pedagogical Sciences and First Deputy Director of NAPS of Ukraine, named Svitlana Kalashnikova, puts in her dissertation a large emphasis on the professional preparation of Ukrainian leaders in a condition of modern social transformation. Kalashnikova explains the need to create a methodology for the future expansion of leadership potential in Ukraine. Kalashnikova states that the ability for professional development for a leader highly relies on one's education: "[…] *професійна підготовка управлінських кадрів спрямована на розвиток управлінців задля підвищення рівня їх професійної компетентності та удосконалення управлінської діяльності"* (Kalashnikova, 2015).

Another interesting point that Kalashnikova emphasises, is the constant self-exploration of the Ukrainian leader. The main purpose of it is to effectively transform his or her personality based on the environment. She also makes an analysis of the five ideal manager characteristics, as introduced by A. Koppin and J. Barrett, namely: character, purposefulness, clarity, determination and interaction. In addition to that, Kalashnikova discusses Slavic experts, such as V. Sheinov, who emphasises the leader's need to have a prospective vision, creativity and intuition. Kalashnikova states that the essential features that correlate with the essence of a good leader include: the integrity of the individual, responsibility for their own behaviour and deeds, spirituality and morality, purposefulness and focus on development. She concludes that the presence of these components of the leadership style allows for a manager to positively influence his or her followers.

Ukrainian leadership YouTube review
In October 2017, Alexandra Alkhimovich, the leader of Luxoft Ukraine (IT company) gave a speech on the topic of Future Leadership in Ukraine. Alexandra presented on the global business sector and its trends that influence the workflow in developing countries. In order to explain her view on the management style that potentially could be improved in Ukraine, Alkhimovich gave her opinion on the on-going domestic problems occurring in the country. At the beginning of the lecture, she mentions four workforce crises: steadily increasing demographics, gender inequality at work, technology development and migration. The demographic problem includes the rising number of people on earth. Alexandra talks about world overpopulation and its direct influence on competition in the employment market. The migration of Ukrainians abroad is also an important factor. That is why, in the case of Luxoft, the company created the global relocation department that takes care of the employees abroad. The third problem is the fewer numbers of female company managers compared to male counterparts. In Alexandra's opinion, this occurs due to the Slavic tradition of women giving up the idea of a possibly triumphant career, for beginning a family. Later, Alkhimovich underlines this characteristic of Ukrainian employment as 'unexploited resources' and 'lost potential'. The last trend mentioned in the lecture that directly influences the leadership style in Ukraine is the speed of technology development. The current era of artificial intelligence has displaced people from production which forces the leader to analyse key factors and

trends, in order to claim a competitive advantage on the market (LvivBusinessSchool, 2017). Alkhimovich puts in plain words two main qualities that will make a person in charge lead the company in Ukraine. The first is avoiding 'appearing ideal' in the eyes of employees. The rising statistic of managers losing trust at work in Ukraine is a big problem, which directly lowers the efficiency of a company. The truth is a great tool in hands of a successful manager. The second mentioned trait of the future leader is to put the mission and values of the company before money-making (Lviv Business School, 2017).

Understanding hierarchy in Ukraine

To understand hierarchy in Ukraine, one should look at the country's history. During the Soviet era, business culture was characterised by autocracy and centralised decision-making. There was a strong vertical hierarchy, which means that the final decisions would be made by the person with the highest authority. Individual obedience was expected, which created a lot of power distance (Grachev, 2003). The traditional Ukrainian workplace environment is built on the idea of the traditional top-down management system (CCBS Survey, 2018). It is strongly believed that the main views and tasks must and will be spread exclusively by the people with the most power in an organisation. It is not rare to fear the boss and to put in an effort to gain the trust of the superiors in order to secure a working place in the company (CCBS Survey, 2018). According to the Hofstede Insights' research, the power distance in Ukraine is equal to 92, which is extremely high (Hofstede Insights, n.d.). The numbers support the idea of the discrepancy between the people with the most and least power, both in formal and informal business environments.

However, after Ukraine gained its independence, the business environment changed. Ukraine entered the international market economy and foreign companies began to penetrate the Ukrainian market, bringing in modern European and American management practices (Conbere & Heorhiadi, 2006). To keep up with the pace of the rapidly changing business environment, Ukrainian companies were forced to move towards a more Western way of doing business, which includes: openness, customer-oriented service and organisational agility (Conbere & Heorhiadi, 2006). It is a less hierarchical system, which was hard for Ukrainians to adapt to. It led to conflicts within organisations, between management and employees. Therefore, enterprises tend to only hire younger people, whose values have not been influenced by the experience of working in the Soviet System (Conbere & Heorhiadi, 2006).

How the Ukrainians achieve leadership empathy

According to Singh (2014), empathy will reduce anxiety and tension in a business environment. When creating positive relationships inside an organisation, it is important to offer encouraging words but also be patient and empathetic (Singh, 2014). Due to the Ukrainian history, there are still businesses with strict hierarchical order and an authoritarian culture. The result of this Ukrainian business culture is a decrease in genuine employee involvement (Croucher, 2010). When trying to achieve leadership empathy in Ukraine, there are certain do's and don'ts to take into account. The statistics of our leadership survey show that the majority of leaders prefer to keep a personal distance from employees, to maintain the right level of respect (CCBS Survey, 2018). Respect towards the culture and language is very important when doing business in Ukraine. Ukrainians who feel respected will respond in helpful and friendly ways.

Plotnytska (21 March 2018) states that leadership characteristics such as empathy are highly appreciated in both young and more senior leaders: "[..] *the ability to hear, understand and share the ambitions of others is the goal of the company's first positions. Empathy has also greatly helped Ukrainian leaders find the best approach to consistently work in a team* [...]" (Plotnytska, 21 March 2018). Moreover, Tsaberiabyi states in the leadership survey: "*Much efforts are spent on growing the level of associates' engagement and well-being which are crucial for high-quality work*" (CCBS Survey, 2018). Nevertheless, Ukrainian negotiations can be quite bureaucratic, as there is a lot of government interference. This can cause frustration for both business partners and is the reason why it is imperative for Ukrainian leaders to have patience. A Ukrainian employee mostly looks up to a leader on the basis of organisational experience and market expertise. They expect their leader to be a powerful decision maker, in combination with thinking in a visionary way (CCBS Survey, 2018).

Uruguay

Anke ten Barge & Andrej Karamešić

Uruguay, officially the Oriental Republic of Uruguay, is a sovereign state in the south-eastern region of South America. The country borders with Brazil and Argentina and has an estimated population of over three million inhabitants. After Suriname, Uruguay is the second-smallest nation in South America. The majority of the population lives in the metropolitan area, with over half living in the capital Montevideo (estimated 1.8 million). Other big cities in Uruguay are Salto and Paysandú (PWC, 2014).
In economic terms, the country lacks any great extremes of wealth or poverty. Most Uruguayans have access to good healthcare, clean water and a healthy diet. Hence, life expectancy in Uruguay is fairly long, at 76 years. The common level of education is high, compared to other neighbouring countries, due to the fact that education is free (Euromonitor, 2017). The largest ethnic group in Uruguay is white Latin Americans. Other minorities include Mestizo and Black Uruguayans. Most Uruguayans are of European origin; these are mainly immigrants from Spain and Italy, who have settled in the country during the colonial period (1516-1811).

How the Uruguayans characterise leaders

In an interview with CCBS, Fernando Iruleguy summarised the qualities, which make a leader in Uruguay exceptional. *"A good leader needs to be humble, educated, fair, a doer instead of a thinker, a risk taker and someone getting involved in activities"* (Iruleguy, 7 April 2018). People have respect for a leader, who is not self-interested or too self-assured, someone who puts the team before him or herself (Iruleguy, 7 April 2018). Moreover, Uruguayan leaders are described as accessible and transparent (Sapelli, 28 March 2018).
Family background is one of the key factors of becoming a leader. Another way of doing so is the symbolic kin system of *Compadrazgo*. In the past, when baptized, the children of rural workers would be given a godfather and/or godmother from the local elite, the so-called *'Compadres'* and *'Comadres'*. This practice is meant to assure that the child would get support and a shot at a good

future. Nowadays, this custom is less common (Scott & Marshall, 2009)
A chairman in agriculture explains that being a leader in Uruguay is not always an easy job to perform. Managers of companies in the private sector have quite a handful of problems to deal with as the market is dynamic and often unpredictable. *"Managers, although their intention is to work on long term strategies, have to continuously change their tactics in response to fast changing circumstances"* (CCBS Survey, 2018).

Survey results and what local respondents say

A large majority of Uruguayan respondents agrees with the statement that a manager should actively spend time on the personal well-being of the team members (CCBS Survey, 2018). This is also confirmed by Fernando Iruleguy, who believes that benevolence is of the most central characteristic that a good leader can have (Iruleguy, 7 April 2018).
Secondly, a large portion of the CCBS respondents in Uruguay agrees that most relationships between a leader and his subordinates are informal. To the question whether it is important to address leaders by mentioning their title, many respondents answer that this is never or hardly ever the case. Respect is very much present in the workplace; however, specific titles, such as director, president and others are not commonly used.
The balance between formal and informal behaviour in Uruguay is largely determined by company culture. As a partner in professional services explains, *"It may depend on the company culture, usually within recently established organisations, a more informal behaviour is shown"* (CCBS Survey, 2018). A chairman of a large local company supports this view by saying: *"It really depends more on age difference and how long you know the person than on position. In general people call each other by their first name"* (CCBS Survey, 2018).
Therefore, studying the company culture and observing how employees address each other is advisable for working in a Uruguayan company. By first testing the water and observing communication, unnecessary, confusing and uncomfortable situations can be avoided.
Furthermore, findings from the CCBS Survey define an excellent leader as a visionary thinker and good listener. Leaders need the right mix of qualities to successfully manage others, among which are: technical competence, organisational experience and market expertise (CCBS Survey, 2018).

Local leadership analysis

In-country literature review

The book *Management, Leadership and Entrepreneurship in Latin America: The Land of Opportunity – the Real Leader in the Global Economy* by Dr Librado Enrique Gonzalez gives an in-depth view on Uruguay's current situation of management, leadership and entrepreneurship. For Gonzalez, Uruguay is exhibiting all the signs of an emerging nation, which places the country at a good point in its historic lifetime (Gonzalez, 2014). Uruguayans attach much appreciation and value to top management characteristics such as enhancement of productivity, honesty and ethical company principles, loyalty, social responsibility, foreseeing market trends and certification (Gonzalez, 2014). An efficient manager, therefore, is proactive in that he or she acts pre-emptively to address a problem before it arises rather than afterwards when that problem has already resulted in losses (Gonzalez, 2014).

The government of Uruguay and its institutions are encouraging people, especially when it comes to entrepreneurship. Where there used to be a lack of funding, nowadays people can get support from different institutions in the form of seed capital, co-financing, start-up support and loans (Gonzalez, 2014). Another important factor is that Uruguay creates initiatives, which promote the entrepreneurial spirit. The country has been placing much importance on establishing a clear identity focused on unison. Therefore, the Uruguayans express that they are highly satisfied with the way that democracy works in their country. Gonzalez (2014) believes that the country is on its way to becoming an influential player in the local and international scene as long as the government keeps supporting and empowering up and coming leaders and entrepreneurs and implementing the correct management styles in its corporations.

Fernando Iruleguy: an Uruguayan leadership scholar

In view of his professional background as a professor of International Trade, Logistics and Supply-Chain Management, we asked Fernando Iruleguy for an interview to understand his perspective on leadership in Uruguay. In addition to being an academic, Iruleguy also owns a company providing corporate services. The majority of his clients are foreigners from Brazil, Europe and India. During our interview, it became clear that Iruleguy thinks of an exceptional Uruguayan leader as someone who is humble. Having a human touch and being genuinely interested in the well-being of the employees is also key to success (Iruleguy, 7

April 2018). Besides, the close relationship between a leader and the employees means that leadership styles and the hierarchy in a company are quite informal, compared to other countries in the region. According to Fernando, one of the major reasons why leadership in Uruguay is less formal is because of the small size of the country. *"Being a small country means that we have a closer relationship with the leader, e.g. the President and the Ministers are close with the people. We don't see the leaders as persons far away"* (Iruleguy, 7 April 2018). As a result, there is little to no strict hierarchy. He explains that hierarchy in Uruguay *"[...] is not so noticeable, that is my belief. There is a bit of hierarchy but this is mostly a flat society, very horizontal, democratic, open and everyone has the same rights"* (Iruleguy, 7 April 2018). Even though Iruleguy does not believe that there is one correct style of leadership, he repeats that being humble is significant and that it is a positive aspect of Uruguayan leadership. Next to being humble and genuine, Iruleguy also stresses the importance of collectivism in Uruguay. *"I think a leader needs to have empathy, someone who puts the team before himself and is ready to sacrifice himself in favour of the team"* (Iruleguy, 7 April 2018).

Santiago Fernández Sapelli: an Uruguayan cross-cultural trainer

Santiago Fernández Sapelli is a public speaker and director of his own company The Orange Attitude Consultancy and Digital Agency. In addition, he is also a Professor of Digital Marketing at Universidad ORT, where leadership is his expertise. During an interview with Sapelli, an interesting view on management and leadership styles in Uruguay was revealed. As a successful businessman, professor Sapelli has had plenty of experience with leaders from all calibres. He has been around long enough to have noticed the change in management styles over the years. In his opinion, Uruguay does not have one specific leadership style but combines the best of all, depending on the line of work. For example, in politics, a different management style is used than in international technological companies. *"I think leadership is fundamental in all aspects of life, not only in the professional field but in every aspect of life. Logically, to run a star company you have to be a good leader, but not all directors are necessarily good leaders"* (Sapelli, 28 March 2018). Sapelli believes in becoming a leader, not being born as one. In his eyes, leaders are made all around and every day. In Uruguay, it is normal to get support from your friends and family when you face difficult decisions while running a business. *"We all need help and support to make difficult decisions to run our businesses. In my case in particular, I turned to my friends and family for that support"* (Sapelli, 28 March 2018). In general,

Uruguayans value leaders that they can relate to: someone who is transparent with his or her employees. A difference in leadership and management styles can be seen in older and more traditional companies. When run by senior managers, a formal environment is customary. This is in contrast with start-ups, where open-door policies prevail. In well-established companies, even people's office spaces are determined by their function within the firm. Younger companies often copy their management style from companies like Google or Facebook, allowing for creative space and an inclusive company culture (Sapelli, 28 March 2018). Uruguayans are good hosts and treat guests with much respect. Having a big ego and inflated sense of overconfidence is not the way to go in Uruguay's business world (Sapelli, 28 March 2018).

In-country leadership bestseller
No Más Pálidas is a bestselling book on Uruguayan leadership, written by Enrique Baliño and Carlo Pacheco. After 22 years of experience as General Manager and President at IBM Uruguay, Enrique Baliño founded his own company, which provides strategic consulting services for other companies. He wrote a book, sharing his experience along the way (BCC Conferenciantes, n.d.)

Local leadership book		
Title	No Más Pálidas	
Author	Quatro actitudes para el éxito	
Publisher	Enrique Baliño & Carlos Pacheco	
Year	CreateSpace	
ISBN	November 2010	

In English, the title translates as *No more Pale- four attitudes for success*. The term *'pale'* is used to describe the way, in which people in Uruguay and Argentina always complain about everything all the time. Baliño sees a successful leader as someone who is positive and a team player. Leaders are exceptional yet normal persons, who continuously work on improving themselves and take responsibility for their actions (No Más Pálidas, n.d.). In addition, a managing director comments: *"No mas Pálidas is about how a leader needs to focus on those variables or problems that the organization can actually change or affect and there is absolutely no sense in allocating resources or spend time in those problems that the organization cannot change (e.g. exchange rate, world prices, etc)"* (CCBS Survey, 2018)

Uruguay leadership YouTube review

One of the most outstanding videos on leadership in Uruguay involves the former president of the country, José Mujica. During an interview with José Mujica, which has gathered over two and a half million views, one thing becomes very clear: he is a very humble man. What is interesting is that he was dubbed 'the humblest president'. During this interview, his thoughts on leading Uruguay to a better future become clear. *"I stand out because my values and way of life reflect those of the society, to which I'm honoured to belong"* (Human, 2015). *"Being the president doesn't matter"* (Human, 2015), with these words José Mujica expresses the clear-headedness with which he views himself. Instead of buying a private jet, which Uruguay does not have, he bought an air ambulance helicopter to help people in need. With these actions he showed that the only thing that matters to him is the well-being of the Uruguayans.

Understanding hierarchy in Uruguay

The Hofstede Country Comparison (Hofstede Insights, n.d) indicates that Uruguay has a relatively high Power Distance. This means that companies have a hierarchical order, in which every employee has a certain place. Nevertheless, as Santiago Fernández Sapelli (28 March 2018) puts it, there are a few factors which determine the level of hierarchy. First of all, it depends on the leadership style and culture of the company. Secondly, there are differences between the hierarchy in an international company versus a local company: international companies tend to be more structured and have more hierarchy than the smaller, local ones. And lastly, it depends on who is in charge. Leaders with seniority in Uruguay are seen as strict, whereas, younger leaders are more transparent and informal (Sapelli, 28 March 2018). Likewise, Fernando Iruleguy's opinion is that hierarchy in Uruguay is mostly informal and that a leader should not only act like a part of the team but really act in the name of the group: *"Be humble, be worried about the well-being of employees, you should talk about your personal life. I know in some countries that is considered weird, but here in Uruguay leaders are open and do not hide their own personal life like family for* example. *Show yourself as a real human, a close person, a father, a brother, a friend"* (Iruleguy, 7 April 2018). In most younger companies, there is little or no personal distance between the leaders and employees. In fact, the relationship is often based on friendship. Titles are not very important and there is no need to address a leader by his or her position. It is even customary to talk to one another on a first name basis. As mentioned in the CCBS Survey: *"It really depends more on age difference and how long you know the person than on position. In general, people call each other by their first name"* (CCBS Survey, 2018).

How the Uruguayans achieve leadership empathy

As mentioned in the previous sections, personal relationships between employees and their leader are essential. Most Uruguayans work to live rather than live to work (Hofstede Insights, n.d.). The fact that the relationship between a leader and employee is considered vital is echoed by Santiago Fernández Sapelli. He explains that, depending on the leadership style in a company, younger company leaders strive to be a 'human leader' and to be accessible and transparent (Sapelli, 28 March 2018). Likewise, a partner in professional services mentions: *"As in the whole world leadership traits have been evolving in recent years, focusing more on employee engagement and satisfaction, team building and morale. They foster reaching company goals, but most importantly securing a respectable position in the marketplace"* (CCBS Survey, 2018). Furthermore, Sofía Scarone, Project Executive, comments: *"Empathy might be the most important skill for a leader because he/she can understand you and how you work and therefore point out the best of you"* (CCBS Survey, 2018).

Bibliography

Bibliography

Abbas, Q., & Yaqoob, S. (2009). Effect of leadership development on employee performance in Pakistan. *Pakistan Economic and Social Review*, 47(2), 269-292. Retrieved from http://pu.edu.pk/images/journal/pesr/PDF-FILES/8 ABBAS Effect of Leadership Development.pdf on 20 March 2018.

Abbasova, N. (2017, February 20). Azerbaijan to meet energy needs of Bulgaria. *Azernews*. Retrieved from https://www.azernews.az/oil_and_gas/109173.html on 6 April 2018.

Achoui, M. M. (2009) Human resource development in Gulf countries: an analysis of the trends and challenges facing Saudi Arabia. *Human Resource Development International*, 12(1), 35-46.

Adegbenro, R. (2018). *2019: Nigeria needs leaders that can drive progress* [Video file]. Retrieved from https://www.youtube.com/watch?v=XmWOu2XUxvs&t=17s.

Adekola, A., & Sergi, B. S. (2016). *Global Business Management: A Cross-Cultural Perspective*. Routledge.

Adeyemi, S. (2015). *Cultural approach to leadership in Nigeria is a problem in Nigeria* [Video file]. Retrieved from https://www.youtube.com/watch?v=UyfivGubeUU&t=75s.

Aguilar, M. (2018). Skype interview. 27 March.

Ahmed, S. (2018). *Economic growth to pick up pace in Pakistan, says World Bank report*. Retrieved from https://www.dawn.com/news/1382184 on 23 February 2018.

Ahonen, J., Anttonen, M., Heikkinen, A., Hätälä, J., Lehtola, J., Nurmilaukas, L., Peltokallio, T., Piekkari, A., Reen, M., Smart, S. & Helsinki School of Economics. (2009). *Doing business in Hungary*. Retrieved from http://epub.lib.aalto.fi/pdf/wp/w471.pdf on 8 March 2018.

Aipoh, S. (2018). Telephone interview. 16 March.

Akhtar, S. (2018). Personal interview. 11 March.

Al-Jibreen, H. (2014). *HR Master Key: A Century in Saudi's Labour Market*. Retrieved from http://www.hrmasterkey.com/2014/03/04/a-century-in-saudis-labor-market/ on 2 April 2018.

Alogaili, K. (2017). *The influence of national culture on leadership styles in Saudi Arabia* (Doctoral thesis). University of Hull.

Alon, I., & Higgins, J. M. (2005). Global leadership success through emotional and cultural intelligences. *Business Horizons*, 48, 501–512.

Alonso-Almeida, M., Perramon, J., & Bagur-Femenias, L. (2017). Leadership styles and corporate social responsibility management: Analysis from a gender perspective. *Business Ethics*, 26(2), 147-161.

Alsubaie, A., & Jones, K. (2017). An overview of the current state of women's leadership in higher education in Saudi Arabia and a proposal for future research directions. *Administrative Sciences, 7*(4), 36. doi:10.3390/admsci7040036.

Amer Qureshi and Qaiser Abbas. (2012, 31 May). *Kuch Khaas: Book Launch: LEADERSHIP INSIGHTS* [Video file]. Retrieved from https://www.youtube.com/watch?v=RArUuhiYh8s.

American University in Bulgaria (AUBG). (2014, 3 September). *Velina Getova - Leadership for a New Era* [Video file]. Retrieved from https://youtu.be/-DmtFlc1WU4.

Amondi, O. B. (2010). Representation of Women in Top Educational Management and leadership Positions in Kenya. *Advancing Women in Leadership, 31*, 57-68.

Andersen, J & Kovac, J. (2013). Why European subordinates trust their managers. *Organizacija*, 45(6), 300-309. Retrieved from https://www.degruyter.com/downloadpdf/j/orga.2012.45.issue-6/v10051-012-0029-x/v10051-012-0029-x.pdf on 19 April 2018.

Aragón-Correa, J. A., García-Morales, V. J., & Cordón-Pozo, E. (2007). Leadership and organizational learning's role on innovation and performance: Lessons from Spain. *Industrial Marketing Management*, 36(3), 349-359.

Ardichvili, A., & Gasparishvili, A. (2001). Socio-cultural values, internal work culture and leadership styles in four post-communist countries: Russia, Georgia, Kazakhstan and the Kyrgyz Republic. *International Journal of Cross Cultural Management*, 1(2), 227-242. Retrieved from http://journals.sagepub.com/doi/abs/10.1177/14705958011206 on 15 February 2018.

Arif, S. (2018). Personal interview. 11 April.

Armenio Rego. (2015). *Aprendendo liderança com o Papa Francisco, com Arménio Rego* [Video file]. Retrieved from https://www.youtube.com/watch?v=Or7Ba9Xpa-4.

Arménio Rego. (2018). Arménio Rego. Retrieved from https://www.researchgate.net/profile/Armenio_Rego on 20 March 2018.

Asimakopoulou, B. (2018). Audio interview. 15 March.

Avolio, B. J., & Gardner, W. L. (2005). Authentic leadership development: Getting to root of positive forms of leadership. *Leadership Quarterly*, 16, 315-338.

Avolio, B., Walumbwa, F., & Weber, T. J. (2009). *Leadership: Current Theories, Research, and Future Directions.* Lincoln: Management Department Faculty Publications.

Back, M. (2012). *Developing a Guide for Internship in Spain. Case: Spain Internship SC* (Master's Dissertation). Retrieved from https://www.theseus.fi/bitstream/handle/10024/39023/Thesis_Mia_Back.pdf?sequence=1&isAllowed=y on 3 March 2018.

Badaracco, J., & Ellsworth, R. (1994). *El liderazgo y la lucha por la integridad*. Bogotá, Columbia: Norma.

Bar-On, R., & Parker, J. D. A. (2000). *The handbook of emotional intelligence.* San Francisco, CA: Jossey-Bass.

Barr, L.I. (2017). *Leadership in Nigeria and the way forward* [Video file]. Nigeria: Wazobia Max. https://www.youtube.com/watch?v=upY6Z16BSSw&t=130s.

Barsby, J. (2017). *Kenya - Culture Smart!: The Essential Guide to Customs & Culture*. London: Kuperard.

Bauer, B. (2007). *Kazakhstan's Economic Challenges: How To Manage the Oil Boom*. Retrieved from https://link.springer.com/article/10.1007/s11300-007-0131-6 on 15 February 2018.

BBC News. (2018). *Greece country profile*. Retrieved from Retrieved from http://www.bbc.com/news/ on 27 February 2018.

BBC News. (3 August 2017). *Ukraine country profile*. Retrieved from http://www.bbc.com/news/world-europe-18018002 on 20 February 2018.

BBC. (2015) *Saudi Arabia Profile Overview*. Retrieved from http://www.bbc.com/news/world-middle-east-14703476 on 22 March 2018.

BBC. (2018, February 19). *Pakistan country profile*. Retrieved from http://www.bbc.com/news/world-south-asia-12965779 on 22 February 2018.

BCC Conferenciantes. (n.d.). *Enrique Baliño*. Retrieved from http://grupobcc.com/speakers/enrique-balino/ on 22 March 2018.

Bendini, R. (2013). *Kazakhstan: Selected trade and economic issues*. Retrieved from http://www.europarl.europa.eu/RegData/etudes/briefing_note/join/2013/522303/EXPO-INTA_SP%282013%29522303_EN.pdf on 5 April 2018.

Benedix, A. (2017, December 17). *Mitarbeiter motivieren: 7 Führungsfehler, mit denen du deine guten Mitarbeiter vergraulst* [Video file]. Retrieved from https://youtu.be/nslQLHSjMLk on 16 April 2018.

Bergmann, A. (1990). Nationale Kultur – Unternehmenskultur [National culture – corporate culture]. Die *Unternehmung*, 44, 360-370.

Bhagat, R. S., & Steers, R. M. (Eds.). (2009). Cambridge handbook of culture, organizations, and work. Cambridge University Press. Retrieved from http://common.books24x7.com.rps.hva.nl:2048/book/id_32058/book.asp on 15 February 2018.

Bobina, M., Sabotinova, D., & Grachev, M. (2017). Women in Bulgarian Management: Cultural Perceptions. *The Journal of Business Diversity*, 17(3), 10-11. Retrieved from https://search-proquest-com.rps.hva.nl:2443/docview/2008872986?accountid=130632 on 10 April 2018.

Borgulya, A., & Hahn, J. (2008). Work related values and attitudes in central and eastern Europe. *Journal for East European Management Studies*, 13(3), 216-238. Retrieved from https://search-proquest-com.rps.hva.nl:2443/docview/232765737?accountid=130632 on 1 March 2018.

Borgulya, I. (2000). A magyar menedzserek és az interkulturális feladatok. *OTKA – kutatási jelentés (Hungarian Managers and Intercultural Tasks. OTKA – Research Report)*, Pécs; PTE. Retrieved from https://www.econstor.eu/bitstream/10419/84048/1/768247403.pdf on 27 February 2018.

Boros-Kazai, A. (2005). Hungary. In R. Frucht (Ed.), *Eastern Europe: an introduction to the people, lands, and culture* (pp. 329-413). Santa Barbara, USA: ABC Clio.

Bosga, R. (2018). Personal interview. 17 April.

Bourantas, D.K. (2005). *Ηγεσία: The road of lasting success*. Kritiki Publishing.

Buch, H., Krummaker, S., & Vogel, B. (2012). *Leadership - Best Practices und Trends* (2nd ed.). Berlin, Germany: Gabler Verlag.

Bulgarian Cultural Institute London. (n.d.). *Curious Facts*. Retrieved from http://www.bcilondon.co.uk/about-us/discover-bulgaria/curious-facts/ on 17 April 2018.

Bulgarian Presidency of the Council of the European Union. (n.d.). *About Bulgaria*. Retrieved from https://eu2018bg.bg/en/about-bulgaria on 17 April 2018.

Burns, J. M. (1978). *Leadership*. New York: Harper & Row.

Businessculture. (2014). *Business Culture in Bulgaria*. Retrieved from http://businessculture.org/eastern-europe/bulgaria/ on 5 March 2018.

Businessculture. (n.d.). *Business culture in Slovenia*. Retrieved from *http://businessculture.org/southern-europe/business-culture-in-slovenia/business-etiquette-in-slovenia/* on 1 March 2018.

Buzady, Z. (2018). Telephone interview. 6 April.

Cakar, U., & Kim, H. (2015). *Paternalistic Leadership in Korean Small and Medium Scale Enterprises: Applicability of a Turkish Paternalism Scale.* Retrieved from https://www.academia.edu/16758443/PATERNALISTIC_LEADERSHIP_IN_KOREAN_SMALL_AND_MEDIUM _SCALE_ENTERPRISES_APPLICABILITY_OF_A_TURKISH_PATERNALISM_SCALE20. on 20 March 2018.

Cappeli, P., Singh, H., Singh, J. V. & Useem, M. (2010). *Leadership Lessons From India.* Retrieved from https://hbr.org/2010/03/leadership-lessons-from-india on 6 March 2018.

Castaño, N., de Luque, M. F. S., Wernsing, T., Ogliastri, E., Shemueli, R. G., Fuchs, R. M., & Robles-Flores, J. A. (2015). El Jefe: Differences in expected leadership behaviors across Latin American countries. Journal of World Business, 50(3), 584-597. Retrieved from https://enriqueogliastri.files.wordpress.com/2013/08/1-el-jefe-leadership-in-latam-jwb-12-6-14_castac3b1o-et-al.pdf on 7 March 2018.

Castillo-Carandang, N. (2018). Skype interview. 21 March.

Castleberry, R. A. (2018). Telephone interview. 12 April.

CCBS Survey. (2016). Worldwide Leadership Survey. In SurveyMonkey online: Amsterdam University of Applied Sciences

CCBS Survey. (2017). Worldwide Leadership Survey. In SurveyMonkey online: Amsterdam University of Applied Sciences.

CCBS Survey. (2018). Worldwide Leadership Survey. In SurveyMonkey online: Amsterdam University of Applied Sciences.

Chhokar, J. S, Brodbeck, F. C., & House, R. J. (Eds.). (2008). *Culture and Leadership Across the World: The GLOBE Book of In-Depth Studies of 25 Societies.* New York, NY: Taylor & Francis Group.

Chhokar, J. S., Brodbeck, F. C., & House, R. J. (Eds.). (2013). *Culture and Leadership Across the World: The GLOBE Book of In-Depth Studies of 25 Societies*. London, England: Routledge.

Chokar, J. S., Brodbeck, F. C. & House, R. J. (Eds.). (2007). *Culture and Leadership Across the World: The GLOBE Book of In-Depth Studies of 25 Societies*. New York: Lawrence Erlbaum Associates.

Chopik, W. J., O'Brien, E., & Knorath, S. H. (2016). Differences in empathic concern and perspective taking across 63 countries. *Journal of Cross-Cultural Psychology*, 48(1), 23-38. Retrieved from http://journals.sagepub.com/doi/abs/10.1177/0022022116673910 on 5 April 2018.

Chou, S. Y. (2017). Millennials in the Workplace: A Conceptual Analysis of Millennials' Leadership and Followership Styles. *International Journal of Human Resource Studies, 2*(2), 71-83. doi:10.5296/ijhrs.v2i2.1568.

CIC Saudi Arabia (2018). *The Saudi-UK Business Forum: Women in Leadership: Empowering Rising Leaders* [Video file]. Retrieved from https://www.youtube.com/watch?v=pdGkyYIC-AA .

CIC Saudi Arabia. (2018, March 8) *The Saudi-UK Business Forum: Women in Leadership: Empowering Rising Leaders* [Video file]. Retrieved from https://www.youtube.com/watch?v=pdGkyYIC-AA.

Ciela. (2018). *Liderstvo / Лидерство*. Retrieved from http://ciela.bg/books/book/liderstvo/2053 on 25 March 2018.

CNN Español. (2015). *Fuerza en Movimiento - Liderazgo Empresarial* [Video file]. Retrieved from https://www.youtube.com/watch?v=Q-jojiCPTQw.

Commisceo Global. (n.d). *Kazakhstan Guide*. Retrieved from Commisceo-global https://www.commisceo-global.com/country-guides/kazakhstan-guide on 20 March 2018.

Commisceo Global. (n.d.). *Intercultural Management: Being a Manager in Pakistan*. Retrieved from https://www.commisceo-global.com/management-guides/pakistan-management-guide on 8 March 2018.

Commonwealth Network. (n.d.). *Pakistan Government*. Retrieved from http://www.commonwealthofnations.org/sectors-pakistan/government/ on 22 February 2018.

Conbere, J. P., & Heorhiadi, A. (2006). Cultural influences and conflict in organizational change innyts new entrepreneurial organizations in Ukraine. *International Journal of Conflict Management*, 17(3), 226-241.

Conrad, M. A. (2013). *Ethical Leadership in Kazakhstan: An Exploratory Study*. Retrieved from https://scholar.valpo.edu/cgi/viewcontent.cgi?article=1072&context=jvbl on 15 February 2018.

Constable, P. (2017, September 09). 'A disaster in the making': Pakistan's population surges to 207.7 million. *Washington Post*. Retrieved from https://www.washingtonpost.com/world/asia_pacific/a-disaster-in-the-making-pakistans-population-has-more-than-doubled-in-20-years/2017/09/08/4f434c58-926b-11e7-8482-8dc9a7af29f9_story.html?utm_term=.e51a8e221b44 on 22 February 2018.

Constitution of the Federal Republic of Nigeria. (n.d.). *Section 304*. Retrieved from http://www.nigerialaw.org/ConstitutionOfTheFederalRepublicOfNigeria.htm#Chapter_8 on 29 March 2018.

Counsil Kenya. (2010). The Constitution of Kenya, 2010. Retrieved from http://www.wipo.int/edocs/lexdocs/laws/en/ke/ke019en.pdf on 20 April 2018.

Cropanzano, R., & Mitchell, M. S. (2005). Social Exchange Theory: An Interdisciplinary Review. *Journal of Management*, 31(6), 874-900. doi:10.1177/0149206305279602.

Croucher, R. (2010). Employee involvement in Ukrainian companies. *International Journal of Human Resource Management*, 21(14), 2659-2676.

Cultural Information. (n.d.). *Kenya*. Retrieved from https://www.international.gc.ca/cil-cai/country_insights-apercus_pays/ci-ic_ke.aspx?lang=eng#cn-6 on 16 March 2018.

Culture Crossing Guide. (n.d). Retrieved from http://guide.culturecrossing.net/basics_business_student_details.php?Id=22&CID=163 on 11 March 2018.

Danish, R. Q., & Usman, A. (2010). Impact of reward and recognition on job satisfaction and motivation: An empirical study from Pakistan. International journal of business and management, 5(2), 159. doi:10.5539/ijbm.v5n2p159.

Daum. (n.d.) *결정적 순간의 리더십*. Retrieved from http://book.daum.net/detail/book.do?bookid=KOR9788965704256 on 11 March 2018.

De Griekse Gids. (n.d.). Retrieved from https://www.grieksegids.nl/griekenland-informatie/bevolking-griekenland.php on 05 April 2018.

Dell, P., & Eriks, F. (2018). E-mail. 26 April.

Derecskei, A. (2016). How do leadership styles influence the creativity of employees? *Society and Economy*, 38(1), 103-118. Retrieved from https://search-proquest-com.rps.hva.nl:2443/docview/1796794623?accountid=130632 on 27 February 2018.

Dimovski, V., Grah, B., Penger, S., & Peterlin, J. (2010). *Authentic Leadership in Contemporary Slovenian Business Environment: Explanatory Case Study of HERMES SoftLab*. Organizacija, 43(5). Retrieved from http://organizacija.fov.uni-mb.si/index.php/organizacija/article/view/359/718 on 10 April 2018.

Dobi, L., Szücs, E., Takács, T., & Matkó, A. (2013). Vezetési stílusok és a szervezeti kultúra kapcsolatának azonosítása egy Magyarországi. *Debreceni Műszaki Közlemények*, pp. 94-111. Retrieved from http://old.eng.unideb.hu/dmk/docs/20132/matko_andrea.pdf on 13 March 2018.

Dolan, S. L., Diez-Pinol, M., Fernandez-Alles, M., Martin-Prius, A., & Martinez-Fierro, S. (2004). Exploratory study of within-country differences in work and life values: the case of Spanish business students. *International Journal of Cross Cultural Management*, 4(2), 157-180.

Dong-A Ilbo, The. (2012). *Korea has biggest gender wage gap among OECD nations*. Retrieved from http://english.donga.com/List/3/all/26/403346/1. on 28 March 2018.

Drucker, P. F. (2001). *The essential Drucker: Selections from the management works of Peter F. Drucker*. New York: HarperBusiness.

Earley, P.C., & Ang, S. (2003). *Cultural Intelligence: Individual interactions across cultures*. Retrieved from https://books.google.nl/books?id=g0PSkiOT8ggC& _r&cad=0#v= &q&f=false on 23 November 2017.

Ehusani, G. (n.d.). *Nigeria and the leadership challenge*. Retrieved from http://www.georgeehusani.org/home/index.php/other-articles/140-nigeria-and-the-leadership-challenge on 21 March 2018.

EIGE. (2013, June 13). *Bulgaria. Gender Equality Index - Country Profiles*, 18-22. Italy: European Institute for Gender Equality. doi:10.2839/9948.

EIGE. (2017, October 10). *Gender Equality Index 2017 - Measuring gender equality in the European Union*, 2005-2015. Italy: European Institute for Gender Equality. doi:10.2839/707843.

Ejimabo, O. N. (2013). Understanding the Impact of Leadership in Nigeria: Its Reality, Challenges, and Perspectives. *SAGE journals*. Retrieved from http://journals.sagepub.com/doi/pdf/10.1177/2158244013490704 on 22 March 2018.

Estes, D. (2012). *An Analysis of Korean and American Leadership Styles in Business*. Retrieved from http://digitalcommons.liberty.edu/cgi/viewcontent.cgiarticle=1277&context=honors on 12 March 2018.

Euromonitor International. (2017). *Business Dynamics: Uruguay*. Retrieved from http://www.portal.euromonitor.com/portal/analysis/tab on 20 March 2018.

Euromonitor International. (2018). *South Korea: Country Profile*. Retrieved from http://www.portal.euromonitor.com.rps.hva.nl:2048/portal/analysis/tab on 20 February 2018.

Eurostat. (2017). *GDP per capita in PPS*. Retrieved from http://ec.europa.eu/eurostat/web/products-datasets/-/tec00114 on 6 April 2018.

Eurostat. (2017). *Tourism statistics*. Retrieved from http://ec.europa.eu/eurostat/statistics-explained/index.php/Tourism_statistics on 19 March 2018.

Facts about Korea. (1991). *New Jersey: Hollym International Corporation*. Retrieved from https://search-proquest-com.rps.hva.nl:2443/docview/212166408?rfr_id=info%3Axri%2Fsid%3Aprimo on 11 March 2018.

Farnsworth-Alvear, A., Palacios, M., & Gómez López, A. M. (2016) *The Colombia Reader: history, culture, politics*. Durham: Duke University Press.

Fei, H., & Wang, M. (2017). Interview CCBS South Korea Sound cloud. 11 April.

Fnac, A. (2018). *Essência da Liderança*. Retrieved from: https://www.fnac.pt/A-Essencia-da-Lideranca-Armenio-Rego/a15533# on 8 April 2018.

Fouad, F. (2013). *Internationalization of Family Businesses in Saudi Arabia*. (Doctoral Thesis). Walden University.

Frauendorfer, D., Schmidt Mast, M., Sanchez-Cortes, D., & Gatica-Perez, D. (2015). Emergent Power Hierarchies and Group Performance. *International Journal of Psychology*, 50(5), 392-396. doi:10.1002/ijop.12102.

Gál, M. (2012). Leadership - Organizational culture: Is there a relationship? *Universitatii Bucuresti Analele Seria Stiinte Economice Si Administrative*, 6, 89-113. Retrieved from https://search.proquest.com/docview/1672863666?accountid=130632 on 13 March 2018.

Galanaki, E., Papalexandris, N., & Chalikias, J. (2009). Revisisting leadership styles and attitudes towards women as managers in Greece: 15 years later. *Gender in Management: An International Journal*, 24(7 & 8).

Gancheva, G. (2014). *How to engage employees according to their age*. Retrieved from https://www.karieri.bg/management/2268532_kak_da_angajirame_slujitelite_spored_vuzrastta_im/ on 6 April 2018.

Gazarian, R. (2015, September 22). The Armenians of Kiev. *Armenian Weekly*. Retrieved from https://armenianweekly.com/2015/09/22/the-armenians-of-kiev/ on 11 March 2018.

Gentry, W.A., Weber, T., & Sadri, G. (2016). *Empathy in the Workplace, A Tool for Effective Leadership*. Retrieved from http://www.ccl.org/wp-content/uploads/2015/04/EmpathyInTheWorkplace.pdf on 26 April 2018.

Ghulam, H., Wan, K., W, I., & Muzhar, J. (2017). Comparability of leadership constructs from the Malaysian and Pakistani perspectives. *Cross Cultural & Strategic Management*, 24(4), 617-644. Retrieved from https://doi.org/10.1108/CCSM-11-2015-0158 on 26 March 2018.

Gielen, R. (2018). Personal interview. 4 April.

Global Affairs Canada. (2017). *Cultural Information - Pakistan | Centre for Intercultural Learning*. Retrieved from https://www.international.gc.ca/cil-cai/country_insights-apercus_pays/ci-ic_pk.aspx?lang=eng on 8 March 2018.

Global Affairs Canada. (2017). Retrieved from https://www.international.gc.ca/cil-cai/country_insights-apercus_pays/ci-ic_ph.aspx?lang=eng#cn-5 on 20 February 2018.

Globe. (n.d.). Global Leadership & Organizational Behavior Effectiveness. Retrieved from http://globeproject.com/results between 3 March and 24 April 2018.

Gonzalez, L. E. (2014). *Management, Leadership and Entrepreneurship in Latin America: The New Land of Opportunity - the Real Leaders in the Global Economy*. Authorhouse.

Gotcheva, N. (2008). A cross-cultural study of leadership styles among executives in Bulgaria and Finland. *International Journal of Human Resources and Management,* 8(3), 246-258. doi:10.1504/IJHRDM.2008.018789.

GOV.UK. (n.d.). *Travelling to Kazakhstan.* Retrieved from https://www.gov.uk/world/kazakhstan#/world/travelling-to-kazakhstan on 5 April 2018.

Grachev, M. V. (2003). Cultural attributes of Russian management. *Advances in International Management*, 15, 159-178.

Greaves, A. (2018). Skype Interview. 30 March.

Greeka. (n.d.). The Greek Islands Specialists. Retrieved from https://www.greeka.com/greece- geography/ on 30 March 2018.

Greenleaf Center for Servant Leadership. (2016). *What is Servant Leadership?* Retrieved from https://www.greenleaf.org/what-is-servant-leadership/ on 12 April 2018.

Gubaidilin, V. (n.d.). *What do most people in Kazakhstan think of Nursultan Nazarbajev?* Retrieved from https://www.quora.com/What-do-most-people-in-Kazakhstan-think-of-Nursultan-Nazarbajev on 23 March 2018.

Guest, S. (2018). Personal interview. 8 March.

Gupta, V., Hanges, P. J., & Dorfman, P. (2002). Cultural clusters: Methodology and findings. *Journal of world Business*, 37(1), 11-15.

Gupta, V., & Singh, S., (2012). How leaders impact employee creativity: a study of Indian R&D laboratories, *Management Research Review*, 36(1), 66-88.

Hamid, S. (2018). *Saad Hamid at YLC'17* [Video file]. Retrieved from https://www.youtube.com/watch?v=mVOIngu2CVU on 22 March 2018.

Hofstede Insights. (n.d.). *Country Comparison*. Retrieved from: https://www.hofstede-insights.com/country-comparison/ between 1 March 2018 and 11 April 2018.

Hofstede, G. & Bond, M. H. (1984). Hofstede's Culture Dimensions An Independent Validation Using Rokeach's Value Survey. *Journal of cross-cultural psychology*, 15(4), 417-433.

Hofstede, G. & Hofstede, G. J. (2005). *Cultures and Organizations: Software of the Mind*. McGraw-Hill.

Hofstede, G. (2001). *Culture's Consequences: Comparing Values, Behaviors, Institutions and Organizations Across Nations* (2nd ed.). Thousand Oaks, California, USA: Sage Publications Inc.

Hofstede, G. (2010). *Cultures and Organizations*. Amsterdam, Nederland: Athenaeum.

Hofstede, G. (2018). *The 6 dimensions of national culture*. Retrieved from https://www.hofstede-insights.com/models/national-culture/ on 11 March 2018.

Hofstede, G., Hofstede, G. J., & Minkov, M. (2010). *Cultures and Organizations: Software of the Mind* (3rd ed.). New York, NY, USA: McGraw-Hill.

Horne, C. M. (2014). *Lustration, Transitional Justice, and Social Trust in Post-Communist Countries: Repairing and Wresting the Ties that Bind.* Retrieved from http://web.b.ebscohost.com/ehost/pdfviewer/pdfviewer?vid=5&sid=368e2315-722b-4ce6-b82c-12f16ea0f13f%40pdc-v-sessmgr01 on 22 March 2018

House, R. J., Hanges, P. J., Javidan, M., Dorfman, P. W., & Gupta, V. (Eds.). (2004). *Culture, leadership, and organizations: The GLOBE study of 62 societies.* Sage publications.

HUMAN. (2015, September 11). *Jose's interview - URUGUAY - #HUMAN* [Video file]. Retrieved from https://www.youtube.com/watch?v=4GX6a2WEA1Q

Hungarian Central Statistical Office. (2017, July 5). *Foreign citizens residing in Hungary by continents, countries, sex. 1 January (1995–)* [Dataset]. Retrieved from https://www.ksh.hu/docs/eng/xstadat/xstadat_annual/i_wnvn001b.html on 21 February 2018.

Hungarian Central Statistical Office. (2017, June 30). *1.1. Population, vital events* (1941–) [Dataset]. Retrieved from https://www.ksh.hu/docs/eng/xstadat/xstadat_annual/i_wnt001b.html on 21 February 2018.

IE Business School. (2013, March 19). *Tango -with IE Professor Margarita Mayo* [Video File]. Retrieved from https://www.youtube.com/watch?v=lkz_uwEQVi8&t=43s on 24 March 2018.

Ignatov, B. (2018). Leadership in Bulgaria with a cross-cultural trainer. (L. Tomov, Interviewer, & L. Tomov, Translator). 2 April.

Inanlou, Z., & Ji-Young, A. (2017). The effect of organizational culture on employee commitment: A mediating role of human resource development in Korean firms. *Journal of Applied Business Research*, 33(1), 87-94. doi:http://dx.doi.org.rps.hva.nl:2048/10.19030/jabr.v33i1.9869.

Incallado, R.B. (2018). Whatsapp interview, 9 April.

India, Ministry of Law and Justice, Legislative Department. (2016). *The Constitution of India.* Retrieved from http://lawmin.nic.in/olwing/coi/coi-english/coi-4March2016.pdf on 27 February 2018.

Ingram, D. (2018). *Transformational leadership vs. transactional leadership definition.* Retrieved from http://smallbusiness.chron.com/transformational-leadership-vs-transactional-leadership-definition-13834.html on 11 March 2018

Instituto Nacional de Estadística. (2017). Retrieved from http://www.ine.es/ on 2 April 2018.

International Labour Organization (ILO). (2016). *Female share of employment in senior and middle management (%): Bulgaria.* Retrieved from http://www.ilo.org/ilostat/faces/oracle/webcenter/portalapp/pagehierarchy/Page27.jspx?indicator=EMP_XFMG_NOC_RT&subject=EMP&datasetCode=A&collectionCode=YI&_adf.ctrl-state=148932plaj_112&_afrLoop=1926989888703601&_afrWindowMode=0&_afrWindowId=148932plaj_5 on 10 April 2018.

Irouma, K. (2018). *The leaders Nigeria needs.* Retrieved from https://www.vanguardngr.com/2018/02/2019-poll-leaders-nigeria-needs/ on 21 March 2018.

Iruleguy, F. (2018). WhatsApp interview. 7 April.

Isado, E. (2018). Telephone interview. 21 March.

Jandi, (2016). 직원들에게 인기 있는 '직장 상사'가 되는 6가지 방법은? [Blogpost]. Retrieved from http://blog.jandi.com/ko/2016/08/19/how-to-lead-cowoker/ on 22 March 2018.

Jumaldildayeva, A. (2016). *SuMo respondent* Retrieved from https://nl.surveymonkey.com/results/SM-NGPZJX9H8/browse/ on 11 March 2018.

Jun, I., Sheldon, P., & Rhee, J., (2010). *Business groups and regulatory institutions: Korea's chaebols, cross-company shareholding and the East Asian crisis.* Retrieved from https://search-proquest-com.rps.hva.nl:2443/docview/761024351?rfr_id=info%3Axri%2Fsid%3Aprimo on 11 March 2018.

Kagema, D. (2018). Responsible Leadership and Sustainable Development in Post Independent Africa: A Kenyan Experience. *The Journal of Values-Based Leadership*, 11(1), Retrieved from http://scholar.valpo.edu/jvbl/vol11/iss1/9 on 23 March 2018.

Kahando, D., Maina, T., & Mweru, C. (2017). An appraisal of financial management practices on the growth of micro enterprise in Kenya. *Journal of Business and Economic Development.* Retrieved from doi:10.11648/j.jbed.20170201.18

Kalashnikova, S. (2015). Theoretical-methodological bases professional preparation for managers-leaders in conditions of modern social transformations.

Kamau, N. (2010). *Women and political leadership in Kenya.* Retrieved from http://ke.boell.org/ on 16 March 2018.

Kaposvari, A. (2018) Telephone call. 4 April.

Katz, L. (2006). *Negotiating International Business - The Negotiator's Reference Guide to 50 Countries Around the World*. North Charleston, South Carolina: BookSurge Publishing.

Kessler, E., & Wong-MingJi, D. (2009). *Cultural Mythology and Global Leadership*. Cheltenham: Edward Elgar Publishing Limited.

Kettner, V. A., & Carpendale, J. I. (2013). Developing gestures for no and year: Head shaking and nodding in infancy. *Gesture, 2*(13), 193-209. doi:10.1075/gest.13.2.04ket.

Khan S. A., & Varshney D. (2013). Transformational Leadership in the Saudi Arabian Cultural Context: Prospects and Challenges. In Rajasekar J., Beh L. S. (eds). *Culture and Gender in Leadership*. Palgrave Macmillan, London.

Khan, M. I. (2015, September 12). Uncommon tongue: Pakistan's confusing move to Urdu. *BBC*. Retrieved from http://www.bbc.com/news/world-asia-34215293 on 22 February 2018.

Khan, S. A. (2018) Skype interview. 28 March.

Khatari, N. (2005). An alternative model of transformational leadership. *Vision*, 9(2), 19-26.

Kicheva, T. (2017). Management of employees from different generations - challenge for Bulgarian managers and HR professionals. *Economic Alternatives* (1), pp. 103-121. Retrieved from http://www.unwe.bg/uploads/Alternatives/Kicheva_ea_en_br_1_2017.pdf on 5 April 2018.

Kihara, A., Ngugi, P., & Ogollah, K. (2016). Influence of leadership characteristics on performance of large manufacturing firms in Kenya. *Journal of Human Resource and Leadership*, 2(2), 64-79. Retrieved from https://www.iprjb.org/journals/index.php/JHRL/article/download/208/265/ on 4 April 2018.

Kihara, P. (2016). Nexus between leadership styles and performance of small and medium manufacturing firms in Kenya. *British Journal of Applied Science & Technology, 18*(3), 1-13, Retrieved from DOI: 10.9734/BJAST/2016/29341.

Kim, T., Lee, D., Wong, N. Y., & Shan. (2016). Supervisor humor and employee outcomes: The role of social distance and affective trust in supervisor. *Journal of Business and Psychology*, 31(1), 125-139. doi:http://dx.doi.org.rps.hva.nl:2048/10.1007/s10869-015-9406-9.

Kim, W., B'lyou, I., & Wang, M. (2017). *Korea, Republic Of*. Amsterdam University of Applied Sciences. 15 February 2018.

Kobia, J. M. (2017). *Between ME and My Exploits*.

Kobia, J. M. (2018). Personal interview. 4 April.

Kong, J. F. (2018). E-mail interview. 6 March.

Kooyers, J. (2015). The United States and Spain: a comparison of cultural values and behaviors and their implications for the multicultural workplace. *Honors Projects*. 399.

Korea 4 Expats. (2012). *Kibun, Nunchi, Inhwa, Harmony*. Retrieved from http://www.korea4expats.com/article-nunchi-kibun-values-norms-korea.html. on 28 March 2018.

Koshal, J. (2005). Application of the construct of service in the context of Kenyan leaders and managers. Retrieved from https://www.regent.edu/acad/global/publications/sl_proceedings/2005/koshal_servant.pdf on 13 April 2018.

Kovacic, H. & Rus, A. (2014). Leadership competences in Slovenian health care. *Slovenian Journal of Public Health*, 51(1), 11-17. Retrieved from *https://www.degruyter.com/view/j/sjph.2015.54.issue-1/sjph-2015-0002/sjph-2015-0002.xml* on 8 March 2018.

KPMG. (2017). *Economic Snapshot*. Retrieved from https://home.kpmg.com/content/dam/kpmg/za/pdf/2017/06/KPMG_Kenya_final.pdf on 22 March 2018.

Krauthammer Magyarország. (2015, 20 October). *Quotes about Leadership: 2. Berta Csonka* [Video file]. Retrieved from https://www.youtube.com/watch?v=YLNLf8BTID0.

Krauthammer Magyarország. (2015, 3 November). *Quotes about Leadership*: 4. Gerhard Fischbach - [Video file]. Retrieved from https://www.youtube.com/watch?v=YikkOeYFyjk.

Krauthammer Magyarország. (2015, 6 October). *Quotes about Leadership: 1. Zsolt Bella - BT Hungary* [Video file]. Retrieved from https://www.youtube.com/watch?v=AQsdaNtnuJY.

Kumar, R., & Sethi, A.K. (2005). *Doing Business in India*. New York: Palgrave MacMillan.

Kvas, A., & Seljak, J. (2014). The effects of education and training on self-esteem of nurse leaders. *Journal of Health Sciences,* 4(2), 97-104. Retrieved from http://www.jhsci.ba/OJS/index.php/jhsci/article/view/156 on 8 March 2018.

Laborinho, J. (2018). Skype interview. 20 March.

Larrahondo, J.C.G. (2018). Personal interview. 23 April.

Lee, E. H. (2018, March 9). *TV Interview on Woman taking on leadership roles, CNN Philippines* [Video file], Retrieved from https://www.youtube.com/watch?v=V9EMXvNOcZ4.

Lew, Y. L., Yu, W., Lee, C., Im, H-B., & Hahn, B. (2018). *Encyclopaedia Britannica: South Korea.* Retrieved from https://www.britannica.com/place/South-Korea. 15 Februari 2018.

Lewis, R. D. (2005). *When cultures collide: Leading across cultures,* third edition. [Books24x7 version] Retrieved from http://common.books24x7.com.rps.hva.nl:2048/book/id_13710/book.asp on 15 February 2018.

Lewis, R. D. (2005). *When Cultures Collide: Leading across Cultures: Leading, Teamworking and Managing Across the Globe* (3rd ed.). London, England: Nicholas Brealey International.

Lewis, R. D. (2006). *When Cultures Collide: Leading Across cultures, Third edition* [Books24x7version] Retrieved from http://common.books24x7.com.rps.hva.nl:2048/toc.aspxbookid13710 on 22 February 2018.

Lewis, R. D. (2006). *When Cultures Collide: Leading across cultures.* Boston: Nicholas Brealey International.

Lewis, R. D. (2016). *6 Leadership Styles Around the World to Build Effective Multinational Teams.* Retrieved from: https://www.crossculture.com/uncategorized/6-leadership-styles-around-the-world-to-build-effective-multinational-teams/ on 8 March 2018

Lewis, R. D., & Gates, M. (2005). *Leading Across Cultures.* Boston: Nicholas Brealey.

Lhabitant, F., & Zoubir, Y. H. (2003). *Doing business in emerging Europe* [Books24x7version] Retrieved from http://common.books24x7.com.rps.hva.nl:2048/book/id_8805/book.asp on 15 February 2018.

Lituchy, T. R., Galperin, B. L., & Punnett, B. J. (2017). *LEAD: Leadership Effectiveness in Africa and the African Diaspora.* New York: Springer Nature.

Llop, R. (2018). *Vision leadership.* Retrieved from: https://www.iftl.eu/quienes-somos on 1 March 2018.

Loránd, C. (2017). *Top ten countries with the largest Hungarian diaspora in the world.* Retrieved from https://www.bocskairadio.org/en/top-ten-countries-largest-hungarian-diaspora-world/ on 5 March 2018.

Low, K. C. P. (2012). *Father leadership in Kazakhstan.* Retrieved from https://link-springer-com.rps.hva.nl:2443/chapter/10.1007/978-3-642-31287-8_8 on 09 March 2018.

LUHDICA. (2015). *Liderança - Estilos de liderança* [Video file]. Retrieved from https://www.youtube.com/watch?v=7GNmqYt4bKM.

Lutz, D. W. (2009). African Ubuntu philosophy and global management. Journal of Business Ethics, 84(3), 313. DOI: 10.1007/s10551-009-0204-z.

LvivBusinessSchool. (2017, 3 October). *Лекція Александри Альхімович: Лідерство майбутнього* [Video File]. Retrieved from https://youtu.be/qhcovFa8Gl4.

Meinolf D., Ariane, B., Child,J., & Nonaka, I. (2001). *Handbook of organizational learning and knowledge* Oxford: Oxford University Press [Books24x7version]. Retrieved from http://common.books24x7.com.rps.hva.nl:2048/book/id_4305/book.asp on 15 February 2018.

Maj, G. (2014). Saudi women making business leadership gains but still trailing peers in other Gulf states. *Financial Post.* Retrieved from http://business.financialpost.com/executive/executive-women/saudi-women-making-business-leadership-gains-but-still-trailing-peers-in-other-gulf-states on 22 March 2018.

Markov, S. (2015, December 7). *Management of different generations - the challenge for HR professionals.* Retrieved from http://jobtiger.tv/hr-industriya/upravlenieto-na-razlichni-pokoleniya-predizvikatelstvoto-pred-hr-profesionalistite on 6 April 2018.

Marquez, R. (2018). LinkedIn messenger. 9 April.

Masigan, J. K. (2016, 26 May). *Web video on what Filipino youth wants from leaders, World Bank* [Video file]. Retrieved from: https://www.youtube.com/watch?v=IrGAIXOr9sY.

Mataen, D. (2012) *Africa- the Ultimate Frontier Market: A Guide to the Business and Investment Opportunities in Emerging markets Africa.* Harriman House. [Books24x7version] Retrieved from http://common.books24x7.com.rps.hva.nl:2048/toc.aspx?bookid=54180 on 14 March 2018.

Maximov, M. (2015, 12 March). *Maxim Maximov* [Video file]. Retrieved from https://www.youtube.com/user/MAXIMCNL.

Mayhew, B. (2011, June 27). *Work Ethics in The Workplace: Generation Differences* [Blog]. Retrieved from https://brucemayhew.wordpress.com/2011/06/27/work-ethics-in-the-workplace-generation-differences/ on 2 March 2018.

Mayo, M. (2018). *Staying Authentic in Leadership and Life.* Londen, England: Bloomsbury.

Mberia, A., & Midigo, R. (2016). Leadership Styles and Employee Job Satisfaction in Public Service in Kenya; Understanding the Gender Factor. *International Journal of Academic Research and Reflection*, 4(6), 2309-405.

McMullan, R. (2018) *The Richest Countries in the World.* Retrieved from https://www.worldatlas.com/articles/the-richest-countries-in-the-world.html on 9 April 2018.

Meijer, A. (2018). Interview. 13 March.

Mellahii, K. (2007). The effect of regulations on HRM: Private sector in Saudi Arabia. *The International Journal of Human Resource Management, 18*(1), 85-99.

Miguel pina e Cunha. (2018). Retrieved from http://www.novasbe.unl.pt/faculty-research/faculty/faculty-members/item/cunha-miguel-pina-e on 17 March 2018.

Millar, R. (2008). *Doing business with India,* Third edition. [Books24x7version] Retrieved from http://common.books24x7.com.rps.hva.nl:2048/toc.aspx?bookid=28381 on 5 April 2018.

Minja, D. (2010). Leadership Practices: A case of selected corporate institutions in Nairobi, Kenya. *Journal of Language, Technology & Entrepreneurship in Africa*, 2(2), 1-30.

Minja, D. (2017). Rethinking ethical leadership in Kenya: adopting a new paradigm. *Journal of Values-Based Leadership*, 10(1). Retrieved from http://scholar.valpo.edu/jvbl/vol10/iss1/5 on 5 April 2018.

Minor CCBS. (2017 February 15). *Leadership Greece - Interview - Panos Xenokostas* [video file]. Retrieved from https://www.youtube.com/watch?v=ZQbt3SC9uG4.

Minor CCBS. (2016 November 29). *Leadership Kazakhstan - interview - Alexander Pakemonov* [Video file]. Retrieved from https://www.youtube.com/watch?v=KOV0Zjypc7o.

Mittal, R., & Dorfman, P. W. (2012). Servant leadership across cultures. *Journal of World Business*, 47(4), 555-570. doi:10.1016/j.jwb.2012.01.009.

Mole, J. (2002). *Mind your manners: managing business cultures in the new global Europe*, third edition. [Books24x7 version] Retrieved from http://common.books24x7.com.rps.hva.nl:2048/book/id_4929/book.asp on 6 March 2018.

Moran, R.T., Harris, P.R., & Moran, S.V. (2011). *Managing cultural differences: global leadership strategies for cross-cultural business success, eighth edition.* [Books24x7 version] Available from http://common.books24x7.com.rps.hva.nl:2048/toc.aspx?bookid=40158.

Moriano, J. A., Molero, F., & Lévy-Mangin, J. P. (2011). Liderazgo auténtico. *Concepto y validación del cuestionario ALQ en España Psicothema*, 23(2), 336-341.

Morris, T., & Cynthia M. P., (1992). Management style and productivity in two cultures. *Journal of International Business Studies*, 23(1), 169-179.

Mueller, W. R., & Meissner, J. O. (2005). What is the meaning of Leadership. A guided tour through a Swiss-German Leadership Landscape, *Academy of Management Proceedings*, 1, 1-6.

Mughal, N. N. (2018). Personal interview. 17 February.

Mujtaba, B. G., Afza, T., & Habib, N. (2011). Leadership Tendencies of Pakistanis: Exploring Similarities and Differences based on Age and Gender. *Journal of Economics and Behavioural Studies*, 2, 199-212. Retrieved from https://www.researchgate.net/publication/233842282_Leadership_Tendencies_of_Pakistanis_Exploring_Similarities_and_Differences_based_on_Age_and_Gender on 6 March 2018.

Muktharova, A. & Medeni, T. (2013). *Schooling and school leadership In Kazakhstan: suggestions for innovative practice.* Retrieved from http://dergipark.gov.tr/download/article-file/257104 on 5 April 2018

Müller, W. R. (1990). Das Schweizerische Führungsselbstverständnis und seine Wirkungen auf die Wettbewerbsfähigkeit [The Swiss self-conception of leadership and its effects on competitiveness]. *Die Unternehmung*, 42, 371-381.

Mwangi, R., Sejjaaka, K., Canny, S., & Maina, M. (2016). Constructs of Successful and Sustainable SME Leadership in East Africa. Retrieved from DOI: 10.13140/RG.2.1.4966.8248

Nairobi Leadership Acadamy. (n.d.). Retrieved from https://www.nla.sc.ke/ on 13 March 2018.

Nations Online. (n.d.). *Pakistan*. Retrieved from http://www.nationsonline.org/oneworld/pakistan.htm on 22 February 2018.

Nedelko, Z., & Brzozowski, M. (2017). *Exploring the influence of personal values and cultures in the workplace.* Hershey: Business Science Reference. Retrieved from http://ebookcentral.proquest.com/lib/[SITE_ID]/detail.action?docID=4816624 on 7 March 2018.

Netherlands Enterprise Agency (n.d.). *Sector information Pakistan*. Retrieved from https://www.rvo.nl/onderwerpen/internationaal-ondernemen/landenoverzicht/pakistan/sectorinformatie on 22 February 2018.

Nikandrou, I., Apospori, E., & Papalexandris, N. (2003). *Cultural and Leadership Similarities and Variations in the Southern Part of the European Union*. Athens: Athens University of Economics and Business.

Nina Castillo-Caradang. (n.d.). Profile [LinkedIn]. Retrieved from https://www.linkedin.com/feed/ on 23 March 2018.

No Más Pálidas. (n.d.). Retrieved from https://nomaspalidas.com/ on 22 March 2018.

Novinite JSC. (2016, December 27). *Russia Covers Nearly 1/3 of Europe's Gas Consumption in 2016*. Retrieved from http://www.novinite.com/articles/178082/Russia+Covers+Nearly+1+3+of+Europe%27s+Gas+Consumption+in+2016 on 6 April 2018.

NTV Kenya. (2017 March 10). *Building good leadership in Kenya & learning how to pay it forward* [Video file]. Retrieved from https://www.youtube.com/watch?v=_WsxMdNIdeA.

O'Connell, J., & Prieto, J. M. (1998). Una lectura vertical de la Investigación Transcultural sobre la dirección de empresa: el caso español. *Revista de Psicológoa del Trabajo y de las Organizaciones*, 1(4), 51-63.

Obi, P. (2018). *Leadership failure, Nigeria's biggest problem*. Retrieved from https://www.vanguardngr.com/2018/02/leadership-failure-nigerias-biggest-problem-peter-obi/ on 21 March 2018.

OEC. (n.d.). *Switzerland*. Retrieved from https://atlas.media.mit.edu/nl/profile/country/che/ on 16 April 2018.

Ogliastri, E. (2012). *El Liderazgo Organizacional En Colombia Un Estudio Cualitativo*. Retrieved from http://conocimiento.incae.edu/~ogliaste/lid%20cual%2000-10.htm on 16 April 2018.

Ogutu, E. (2014). Retrieved from https://www.standardmedia.co.ke/evewoman/article/200012235 8/pastormbevi-sharpening-boys-to-men on 23 March 2018.

Ojokuku R. M., Odetayo T. A., & Sajuyigbe A. S. (2012). Impact of Leadership Style on Organizational Performance: A Case Study of Nigerian Banks. *American Journal of Business and Management,* 1(4), 202-207.

Okombo, O., Kwaka, J., Muluka, B., & Nyabuto, B. (2011). *Challenging the Rulers: A Leadership Model for Good Governance*. Nairobi: East African Educational Publishers.

Okoye, O. (2018). LinkedIn interview. 5 April.

Oloko, M., & Ogutu, M. (2012). Influence of Power Distance on Employee. *Education Research Journal*. Retrieved from http://citeseerx.ist.psu.edu/viewdoc/download?doi=10.1.1.913.6121&rep=rep1&type=pdf on 25 March 2018.

OWNO. (2015). *One World - Nations Online*. Retrieved from http://www.nationsonline.org/oneworld/bulgaria.htm on 16 March 2018.

Páez, I. & Salgado, E. (2016). When deeds speak, words are nothing: a study of ethical leadership in Colombia. *Business Ethics: A European Review*, 25(4), 538-555. Retrieved from http://dx.doi.org/10.1111/beer.12130 on 20 March 2018.

Pandey, V. (2018) Zoom interview. 16 March.

Pavlushenko, T. (2018). *All leaders - unusual Everyone has the unusual anomaly Look..!*. Retrieved from http://biz.liga.net/hr/all/stati/3725338-vse-lidery-neobychnye-v-vsekh-est-anomalii-ishchite-neobychnykh-.htm on 10 March 2018.

Pfajfar, G., Uhan, M., Fang, T., & Redek, T. (2016). Slovenian business culture–How proverbs shape dynamic leadership styles. *Journal of East European Management Studies*, 21(4), 433-457. Retrieved from http://www.jstor.org/stable/44111959 on 1 March 2018.

Pfister, G. P. (2018), Telephone interview, 13 April.

Pietrzyk, M. (2017). *Worldwide leadership Survey*. In SurveyMonkey online: Amsterdam University of Applied Sciences.

Plotnytska, S. (2018). Skype interview. 21 March.

Pradhan, S., & Pradhan, R. K. (2015). An Empirical Investigation of Relationship among Transformational Leadership, Affective Organizational Commitment and Contextual Performance. *Vision*, 19(3), 227-235.

Prevodnik, M. & Biloslavo, R. (2009). Managers and leaders in organizations of a post-transition economy. *Organizacija*, Volume 42, pp. 87-94. Retrieved from *https://www.degruyter.com/downloadpdf/j/orga.2009.42.issue-3/v10051-009-0006-1/v10051-009-0006-1.pdf* on 19 April 2018.

Prieto, J. M. (1989). Liderazgo como enredo en Ja empresa española. *Boletin. de Estudios Económicos*, 14(136), 35-46.

Pucko, D. & Cater, T. (2011). Cultural dimensions and leadership styles perceived by future managers: differences between Slovenia and a cluster of central European countries. *Journal of Management, Informatics and Human Resources*, 44(4), 89-99. Retrieved from *https://www.degruyter.com/view/j/orga.2011.44.issue-4/v10051-011-0009-6/v10051-011-0009-6.xml* on 8 March 2018.

PWC. (2014). *Doing Business in Uruguay*. Retrieved from https://www.pwc.de/de/internationale-maerkte/assets/doing-business-in-uruguay.pdf on 2 April 2018.

Qasim Ali Shah. (2015 July 8). *What is Leadership? & What Makes a Good Leader* [video file]. Retrieved from https://www.youtube.com/watch?v=qDiEc9F6Iss.

Quesada, C., Pineda-Herrero, P., & Espona, B. (2011). Evaluating the efficiency of leadership training programmes in Spain. *Procedia - Social and Behavioral Sciences*, 30, 2194-2198.

Qureshi, A. & Abbas, Q., (2016). *Leadership Insights*. Lahore: Possibilities Publications.

Radio Free Europe/Radio Liberty. (2017, November 24). *Tymoshenko Says Ukraine's Leaders Not Living Up to 'European Values'* [Video file]. Retrieved from https://www.youtube.com/watch?v=ftjVOPuwbIA on 2 April 2018.

Rahim, M. A., & Marvel, M. R. (2011). The role of emotional intelligence in environmental scanning behavior: A cross-cultural study. *Academy of Strategic Management Journal*, 10(2), 83.

Rakuten kobo. (n.d.). Retrieved from https://www.kobo.com/ww/nl/ebook/kirpichi?changeLanguage=True on 23 March 2018.

Raul Yepes, A. (2016). *Por otro camino, de regreso a lo humano. AGUILAR*. Retrieved from https://www.inspyra.co/single-post/2017/08/09/Por-otro-camino-de-regreso-a-lo-humano on 22 March 2018.

Ravikumar, T. (2013). A study on the impact of teamwork, work culture, leadership and compensation on engagement level of employees in MSMEs in India. *International Journal of Advance Research in Management and Social Sciences,* 2(8), 175–185.

Reyes, R. (2013). Developing a Filipino brand of leadership, *Business Inquirer*. Retrieved from http://business.inquirer.net/104623/developing-a-filipino-brand-of-leadership on 23 March 2018.

Rijksdienst voor Ondernemed Nederland. (n.d.). Retrieved from https://www.rvo.nl/onderwerpen/internationaal-ondernemen on 30 March 2018.

Robin Sharma. (n.d.). Retrieved from: https://www.robinsharma.com/books on 20 March 2018.

Romero, E. J. (2004). *Latin American Leadership: El Patron & El Lider Moderno*. Bingley: Emerald Publishing Group.

Roshupkina, S. (2018, March 01). *Business needs new heroes. How to find an enterprising leader?* Retrieved from http://www.liga.net/opinion/370662_biznesu-nuzhny-novye-geroi-kak-nayti-predpriimchivogo-lidera.htm on 11 March 2018.

Ruben Llop. (2016, May 11). *Business Leadership* [Video file]. Retrieved from https://www.youtube.com/watch?v=KtQ27rPVOeQ .

Ruben Llop. (2016, November 13). *Individual Change* [Video file]. Retrieved from https://www.youtube.com/watch?v=UedFnicOV5c.

Ruben Llop. (2016, November 16). *Strategic Change* [Video file]. Retrieved from https://www.youtube.com/watch?v=hufXOXLWfgM&t=52s.

Rueda Laguna, G. J. (2016). *El liderazgo en Colombia: Un análisis de la investigación empírica en contextos organizacionales.* Bogotá: Universidad del Rosario.

Santos, A. (Director). (2015). *South Korea-Business Culture* [Video file]. Retrieved from https://www.youtube.com/watch?v=17YSRRJBkzE&t=66s.

Sapelli, S. F. (2018). Skype interview. 28 March.

Savery, A. (2012). *Ukraine.* London, United Kingdom: Franklin Watts.

Schweitzer, S. & Alexander, L. (2015). *Access to Asia: your multicultural guide to building trust, inspiring respect, and creating long-lasting business relationships.* [Books24x7 version] Available from http://common.books24x7.com.rps.hva.nl:2048/toc.aspx?bookid=82370.

Scott, J., & Marshall, G. (2009). *A dictionary of Sociology* (3rd ed.). Oxford University Press, USA. doi:10.1093/acref/9780199533008.001.0001

Segal, J. (2012). *Culture-Effective Leadership.* Retrieved from https://ateneo.edu/news/features/role-culture-effective-leadership on 23 March 2018.

Sharma, T. (2017, October 09). *Leadership styles in India* [Video file]. Retrieved from https://www.youtube.com/watch?v=csTNbVUSQyc.

Shiryaevskaya, A. (2016, December 28). Russian Gas. *Bloomberg.* Retrieved from https://www.bloomberg.com/quicktake/russian-gas on 6 April 2018.

Shopov, I (Шопов И. (2017). Мениджърско Поведение и Фирмена Култура. *New Knowledge Journal of Science / Novo Znanie,* 6(1), 39-49.

Simosi, M., & Xenikou, A. (2010). The role of organizational culture in the relationship between leadership and organizational commitment: an empirical study in a Greek organization. *The International Journal of Human Resource Management,* 21(10), 1598-1616.

Singh, N., & Krishnan, V. R. (2005). Towards Understanding Transformational Leadership India: A Grounded Theory Approach. *Vision,* 9(2), 5-17.

Singh, P. (2014). Employees use of empathy to improve their job behaviour. *International Business & Economics Research Journal,* 13(3), 559-610.

Sinha, J. B. P. (1984). A Model of Effective Leadership Styles in India. *International Studies of Management & Organization,* 14(2/3), 86-98.

Sinha, J. B. P. (2008). *Culture and Organizational Behavio*r. New Delhi: Sage.

Sítima L. (2016). *LEADERS Handbook: A Mudança Começa e Acaba nas Pessoas.* LEADERS Model.

Smith, P. B., Dugan, S. & Trompenaars, F. (1996). *National culture and the values of organizational employees.* Retrieved from http://mentalite.ro/content_docs/exploring_mentality/research_papers/Peter%20B%20Smith,%20Shaun%20Dugan%20-%20National%20culture%20and%20the%20values.pdf on 9 March 2018.

Sood, D. (2018). Zoom interview. 18 March.

Southernton, D. (2013). *Working for Korea Inc: Shift in Korean Management Styles* [Video file]. Retrieved from https://www.youtube.com/watch?v=OHilmaWZVUw.

Suutari, V. & Riusala, K. (2001). *Leadership styles in Central Eastern Europe.* Retrieved from https://www.researchgate.net/publication/223871365_Leadership_styles_in_Central_Eastern_Europe_Experiences_of_Finnish_expatriates_in_the_Czech_Republic_Hungary_and_Poland on 10 March 2018.

Sydoryak, M. (2018). Skype interview. 16 March.

Szabo, D. G. (2018) Skype interview. 6 April.

Szalay, G. (2002). *Arbeit und Kommunikation in deutsch – ungarischen Teams.* Budapest: Goethe Institut Inter Nationes, Deutsch-Ungarische Industrie- und Handelskammer.

Szalay, G. (2015). *Arbeit und Kommunikation in deutsch-ungarischen Teams,* 1-7. Retrieved from http://www.ssoar.info/ssoar/handle/document/45131 on 8 March 2018.

Taneva, A. (2018). Leadership in Bulgaria with a leadership scholar. (L. Tomov, Interviewer, & L. Tomov, Translator). 6 April.

The Observatory of Economic Complexity (OEC). (2016). *Hungary*, Retrieved from https://atlas.media.mit.edu/en/profile/country/hun/ on 12 April 2018.

The Orange Files. (N.D.). *The Principality of Hungary.* Retrieved from https://theorangefiles.hu/the-principality-of-hungary/ on 5 March 2018.

The Schweizer Kader Organisation. (2018, February 11). *Leadership the Swiss Way - Olga Feldmeier* [Video file]. Retrieved from https://www.youtube.com/watch?v=bvdJHtCOZ2o.

The Schweizer Kader Organisation. (2018, February 11). *Leadership the Swiss Way - Bernhard Heusler* [Video file]. Retrieved from https://www.youtube.com/watch?v=HuosWt_g-oU.

The Schweizer Kader Organisation. (2018, February 11). *Leadership the Swiss Way - Mimi Mollerus* [Video file]. Retrieved from https://www.youtube.com/watch?v=n0_vU_5sRrc.

The Schweizer Kader Organisation. (2018, February 11). *Leadership the Swiss Way - Eva Jaisli* [Video file]. Retrieved from https://www.youtube.com/watch?v=ykoTGMyeFZA.

The Schweizer Kader Organisation. (2018, February 11). *Leadership the Swiss Way - Henri B Meier* [Video file]. Retrieved from https://www.youtube.com/watch?v=3GrEG7fsnYs.

The World Bank Group. (2018). *World Development Indicators - Bulgaria*. Retrieved from http://databank.worldbank.org/data/reports.aspx?source=2&country=BGR# on 18 March 2018.

The World Bank Group. (2018, January 3). *Country Profile: Bulgaria*. Retrieved from The World Bank: http://databank.worldbank.org/data/views/reports/reportwidget.aspx?Report_Name=CountryProfile&Id=b450fd57&tbar=y&dd=y&inf=n&zm=n&country=BGR

The World Bank. (n.p.). *The World Bank*. Retrieved from https://data.worldbank.org/indicator/NY.GDP.MKTP.KD.ZG?locations=IN on 27 February 2018.

Tipu, S. A. A., Ryan, J. C., & Fantazy, K. A. (2012). Transformational leadership in Pakistan: An examination of the relationship of transformational leadership to organizational culture and innovation propensity. *Journal of Management & Organization, 18*(4), 461-480. doi:10.5172/jmo.2012.997.

Tolymbek, A. (2007). *Political Leadership Style in Kazakhstan*. (Thesis). Retrieved from https://etd.ohiolink.edu/.

Tomalin, B., & Nicks, M. (2012). *The world's business cultures and how to unlock them*. Oxfordshire, England: Thorogood.

Mind Tools. (n.d.). *Hofstede's Cultural Dimensions*. Retrieved from https://www.mindtools.com/pages/article/newLDR_66.htm on 7 March 2018.

Torres, E. T. (2015). *Perceived managerial and leadership effectiveness in Colombia*. Bingley: Emerald Group Publishing Limited.

Treichel, D. (2018). Telephone interview. 27 March.

Trivellas, P., & Reklitis, P. (2014). Leadership competencies profiles and managerial effectiveness in Greece. *Procedia Economics and Finance, 9*, 380-390.

United Nations. (2017). *World Population Prospects: The 2017 Revision*. Retrieved from https://esa.un.org/unpd/wpp/Publications/Files/WPP2017_KeyFindings.pdf on 20 February 2018.

Valsania, S. E., Léon, J. A., Alonso, F., & Cantisano, G. (2012). Authentic leadership and its effect on employees' organizational citizenship behaviours. *Psicothema, 24*(4), 561-566.

Vassiliadis, S., & Vassiliadis A. (2013). *The Greek Family Businesses and the Succession Problem*. Thessaloniki, Greece: Thessaloniki Institute of Technology, Department of Accountancy.

Velez-Ocampo, J., & Gonzalez-Perez, M. A. (2015). International expansion of Colombian firms: Understanding their emergence in foreign markets. *Cuadernos de Administración, 28*(51), 189-215.

Videoinfographs. (Director). (2013). *Doing Business with Koreans* [Video file]. Retrieved form https://www.youtube.com/watch?v=u1wGgzWTDNY&t=2s.

Vodja. (n.d.). Retrieved from http://www.vodja.net/index.php?title=knjiga-o-vodenju&pb=1 on 1 March 2018.

Wambui, T., Wangombe, J., & Jackson, S. (2013). Managing workplace diversity: a Kenyan perspective. *International Journal of Business and Social Science*. Retrieved from http://ijbssnet.com/journals/Vol_4_No_16_December_2013/19.pdf on 13 March 2018.

Warburton, K. (2017a). *World Business Culture, Delivering Connections. Business Culture in Greece*. Retrieved from https://www.worldbusinessculture.com/country-profiles/greece/culture/ on 13 March 2018.

Warburton, K. (2017b). *World Business Culture: Business Culture in Nigeria*. Retrieved from https://www.worldbusinessculture.com/country-profiles/nigeria/culture/ on 21 April 2018.

Warburton, K. (2018). *World Business Culture: Saudi Arabian Management Style*. Retrieved from https://www.worldbusinessculture.com/country-profiles/saudi-arabia/culture/management-style/ on 20 March 2018.

Whitley, R. (1999). *Divergent Capitalisms: The Social Structuring and Change of Business Systems*. Oxford: Oxford University Press.

Wong, S. J. (2018). Personal inteview. 18 April.

Shim, W. S., & Steers, R. M. (2001). The entrepreneurial basis of Korean enterprise: Past accomplishments and future challenges. *Asia Pacific Business Review*, 7(4), 22-43.

World Bank Group. (2017). *Doing Business in Colombia 2017*. Retrieved from http://www.doingbusiness.org/~/media/WBG/DoingBusiness/Documents/Subnational-Reports/DB17-Colombia-Overview-English.PDF on 23 April 2018.

World Culture Encyclopaedia. (n.d.). *Pakistanis*. Retrieved from http://www.everyculture.com/wc/Norway-to-Russia/Pakistanis.html on 22 February 2018.

Worldbank. (2016). *Country Profile (Hungary)*. Retrieved from http://databank.worldbank.org/data/views/reports/reportwidget.aspx?Report_Name=CountryProfile&Id=b450fd57&tbar=y&dd=y&inf=n&zm=n&country=HUN on 12 April 2018.

Yan, J., & Hunt, J. G. (2005). A cross cultural perspective on perceived leadership effectiveness. *International Journal of Cross Cultural Management*, 5, 49–66.

Yoon, H. J. (2012). Predicting employee voice behavior: an exploration of the roles of empowering leadership, power distance, organizational learning capability, and sense of empowerment in Korean organizations. Retrieved from https://search.proquest.com/docview/1027141306?accountid=130632 on 23 March 2018.

Zahariev, E. (Захариев). (2016). Descriptive analysis of corporate culture following the changes. *New Knowledge Journal Of Science / Novo Znanie*, 5-3.

Zárate Torres, A., & Matviuk S. (2012). Inteligencia emocional y prácticas de liderazgo en las organizaciones Colombianas. Retrieved from http://www.scielo.org.co/pdf/cuadm/v28n47/v28n47a08.pdf on 23 March 2018.

Zonis, M., Lefkovitz, D., & Wilkin, S. (2003). *The kimchi matters: Global business and local politics in a crisis-driven world*. Agate Publishing. Retrieved from http://common.books24x7.com.rps.hva.nl:2048/book/id_24916/book.asp on 15 February 2018.

Zubko, K. C. & Sahay, R. R. (2010). *Inside the Indian business mind: a tactical guide for managers*. Retrieved from http://common.books24x7.com.rps.hva.nl:2048/toc.aspx?bookid=44087 on 20 March 2018.

Драч, I. (2015). Leadership and teamwork in the mangement of educational institution. *ScienceRise, 21*(7), 63-67.

기원, 신. (2013). 논어와 맹자에서 배우는 리더십. *Dongyang Daily News*. Retrieved from http://www.dynews.co.kr/news/articleView.html?idxno=199410 on 22 March 2018.

Selected previous CCBS editions

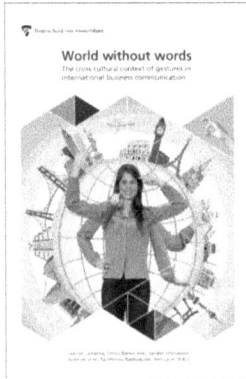

World without words
The cross-cultural context of
gestures in international business
2012, HvA CCBS minor
ISBN 978-90-79646-11-1

World-wide workforce
An intercultural benchmark of
global recruiting practices
2015, HvA CCBS minor
ISBN 978-90-79646-25-8

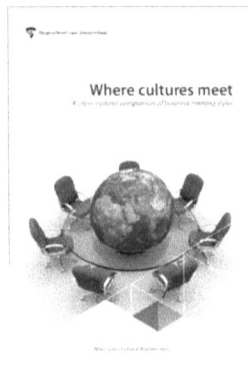

Where cultures meet
A cross-cultural comparison of
business meeting styles
2013, HvA minor CCBS
ISBN 978-90-79646-17-3

www.ingramcontent.com/pod-product-compliance
Lightning Source LLC
Chambersburg PA
CBHW050120210326
41519CB00015BA/4041